"Using plain language and examples from real cases, this valuable new book breaks down complicated legal issues into more clearly understood components and provides useful advice on how creators can best protect their works and careers. Drawing upon decades of experience, the book describes common business practices and provides practical advice for negotiations. Importantly, the book also discusses how best to protect creative work as others exploit it on the Internet without permission, credit or compensation."

—**HELEN E. FREEDMAN**, Justice of the Appellate Division of New York Supreme Court (retired)

"The term 'creative type' carries with it an implicit connotation that we authors and artists are good at creating, but not so good at navigating the legal and financial side of our business. I'm here to tell you that is absolutely correct, and that's why I'm so grateful for a foolproof guide like this one to help show the way."

—**WILLIE GEIST**, host of NBC's *Today* & MSNBC's *Morning Joe*, bestselling author

"Everything you ever wanted to know about copyright but were too intimidated to ask! This is a must-have for all creators who wish to protect the intellectual property interest in their work and better understand the laws that govern those rights. Written in a straightforward and understandable form, this book addresses a wide range of subjects of concern to creators, from libel and privacy issues, to rights in cyberspace, through contracts and other business and tax matters."

—**MICKEY H. OSTERREICHER**, general counsel, National Press Photographers Association (NPPA)

"For authors and artists, for creative people of all stripes and convictions, this book goes to the heart of the matter—or the hearts of the matter, as the case may be—and provides a clear, concise and *essential* guide to the care and protection of the results of the creative process, with the basics as well as the caveats and exception carefully explained."

—**JAMES A. FOX**, senior vice president and general counsel (retired), HarperCollins Publishers

"For over 40 years, Ken Norwick has been my go-to lawyer for all matters involving the law of libel, copyright, obscenity, contracts and the rights of authors and artists. This book makes his learning and experience available to everyone. It does not provide legal advice in particular situations; you'll need a lawyer for that. But for a clear, plain language, easy-to-read explanation of the law affecting the rights of authors, painters, photographers, etc., you won't do better. And it's even fun to read."

—**IRA GLASSER**, author, activist and former executive director of the American Civil Liberties Union

"At a time when writers and artists need all the backbone they can summon, Ken Norwick's accessible, savvy legal primer is a shot of high-grade, concentrated calcium."

—**DAVID MARGOLICK**, author, contributing editor to *Vanity Fair* magazine and former law correspondent for the *New York Times*

"The contract—the binding agreement between the writer and the publisher—is the backbone of the relationship between the two. It provides, in effect, for the best-case and the worst-case scenarios for the author. Understanding the contract is essential for any writer. This book very clearly and thoughtfully lays out the basics of this agreement between creator and publisher and is a 'must-read' for any aspiring artist who contemplates publishing his or her work."

—**GAIL HOCHMAN**, president of the Association of Authors' Representatives

PAGE STREET
PUBLISHING CO.

Copyright © 2017 Kenneth P. Norwick

First published in 2017 by
Page Street Publishing Co.
27 Congress Street, Suite 105
Salem, MA 01970
www.pagestreetpublishing.com

Distributed by Macmillan, sales in Canada by The Canadian
Manda Group.

21   20   19   18   17   1   2   3   4   5

ISBN-13: 978-1-62414-449-3
ISBN-10: 1-62414-449-7

Library of Congress Control Number: 2017909669

Cover and book design by Page Street Publishing Co.

Printed and bound in the United States

THE

LEGAL GUIDE

FOR

WRITERS,
ARTISTS
AND OTHER
CREATIVE PEOPLE

PROTECT YOUR WORK AND UNDERSTAND THE LAW

KENNETH P. NORWICK
WITH COOPER KNOWLTON

CONTENTS

INTRODUCTION

This book is a revised, expanded, and updated edition of *The Rights of Authors, Artists and Other Creative People*, co-authored by Kenneth P. Norwick and Jerry Simon Chasen, that was published in 1992 as part of the American Civil Liberties Union's acclaimed "Rights Of . . ." series. And although much of that earlier book remains accurate and has been carried forward into this one, the ever-changing nature of the law and the publishing, communications, and entertainment industries has required substantial revisions to that book. Most obviously, while that book had barely a mention of "websites" and "the Internet," this book has a whole separate chapter devoted to the "cyber" revolution. It is our hope and intention that this book is as accurate, reliable, and accessible as we could make it for readers in the second decade of the twenty-first century.

Because this book is titled *The Legal Guide for Writers, Artists and Other Creative People*, a few disclaimers are necessary. First, although portions of the book should prove useful to all creative people, the book does not address the legal rights and problems of all creators. Of necessity, lines had to be drawn and categories of creators excluded. Thus, the book does not deal separately with performing artists, those who compose or arrange music, or choreographers or directors, among others. Instead, the book concentrates on those who write articles, books, plays, and motion pictures and those who create works of visual art. As a shorthand, the book refers to all such people as "creators."

Second, the book does not purport to provide the last word on most of the issues it discusses. Especially where the applicable law can vary markedly from state to state, such an undertaking would have been impossible. Instead, the book attempts to provide an introduction to and an overview of the law applicable to the creators to whom it is addressed.

Readers who are confronted with specific legal problems may well find guidance in this book but should nevertheless obtain the assistance of a lawyer familiar with the applicable law in resolving those problems. This book does not contain footnotes or legal citations, but readers wishing to further pursue the law discussed in the book are invited to request further guidance from the authors by writing them at guide@norwickschad.com.

CHAPTER 1

THE CONSTITUTIONAL FOUNDATION

The Constitution of the United States is not only "the supreme law of the land"; it is also the original source of all other law in this country. In Article I, for example, the Constitution spells out the "legislative powers" that are vested in Congress. It is this article that grants to Congress the principal power to enact the laws that ultimately affect the business and personal lives of all of us. And in the Bill of Rights, the Constitution sets forth the fundamental rights and freedoms of all people in this country, rights and freedoms that cannot be denied or abridged by Congress in its laws or by any other branch or level of government.

Unlike most groups or categories of Americans who do not find specific reference to their callings in the Constitution, creative people are doubly blessed: They can point to two separate, and important, references to their activities in the Constitution. Indeed, these two constitutional provisions establish the foundation for the most important legal rights of all creative people.

The first reference, in Clause 8 of Section 8 of Article I, grants Congress the legislative power "to promote the progress of science and useful arts, by securing for limited times to authors and inventors the exclusive right to their respective writings and discoveries."

This clause has empowered Congress to enact copyright laws, which have provided creative people the essential protection they need to continue to create since the first Congress. And although the clause refers only to "authors" and "writings," it is clear that, as the Supreme Court has put it, the copyright clause "may be interpreted to include any physical rendering of the fruits of creative, intellectual, or aesthetic labor." However, as will be discussed in Chapter 2, it is clear that in the copyright laws it has passed, Congress has not protected all the fruits of such labor that it might have.

The second reference to the activities of creative people is in the First Amendment, which provides that "Congress shall make no law . . . abridging the freedom of speech, or of the press." Especially because it is now clear that this provision applies as fully to state and local governments as it does to the federal government, it is easy to agree with the Supreme Court that the First Amendment is "the matrix, the indispensable condition, of nearly every other form of freedom."

The scope of the First Amendment is extensive. Most obviously, it applies to speech and writings on "political" matters. As former Justice Hugo L. Black put it: "In the First Amendment the Founding Fathers gave the free press the protection it must have to fulfill its essential role in our democracy. The press was to serve the governed, not the governors. The Government's power to censor the press was abolished so that the press would remain forever free to censure the Government."

Perhaps of equal importance to most creators, it is clear that the First Amendment is not limited to "political speech." As the Supreme Court confirmed in a major decision: "Entertainment, as well as political and ideological speech, is protected; motion pictures, programs broadcast by radio and television and live entertainment, such as musical and dramatic works, fall within the First Amendment guarantee."

Read literally, the First Amendment prohibits any law that would abridge the "freedom of speech, or of the press," which presumably includes all the creations of all authors and artists. But if anything is clear about the meaning of those words, it is that they do not mean what they seem to say and that the First Amendment has never been construed as "absolute" in its force and effect. Instead, as will be discussed more fully in Chapters 2 and 3, the First Amendment does not necessarily protect all speech and writings. Nevertheless, it and the copyright clause, along with the laws they have engendered, are the sources and bulwarks of the most fundamental rights of all creators.

There is at least a potential conflict between the copyright clause and the First Amendment. Thus, the latter's prohibitions could be read to encompass the freedom to write or speak whatever one wishes, including the writings of others, while the copyright clause makes clear that Congress can prevent such borrowing. As a leading authority on copyright has posed the dilemma: "Does not the Copyright Act fly directly in the face of [the First Amendment's] command? Is it not precisely a 'law' made by Congress which abridges the 'freedom of speech' and 'of the press' in that it punishes expressions by speech and press when such expressions consist of the unauthorized use of material protected by copyright?"

Somewhat surprisingly, the courts have not found it necessary to determine directly whether these two constitutional provisions conflict. However, it is generally assumed that if and when that effort becomes necessary, the courts will not find that the legal protections afforded creators by copyright laws violate the First Amendment but will reconcile whatever conflict exists. Indeed, many courts have at least implicitly done so through the "fair use" exception built into copyright law, referring to the constitutional purpose of the copyright clause—to promote knowledge—and by adhering to the well-established rule that copyright does not protect "ideas" but only "the particular selection and arrangement of ideas, as well as a given specificity in the form of their expression."

It seems clear that creators will continue to be able to claim the protection of both the copyright law and the First Amendment. We shall now turn to the rights afforded under copyright law.

·

CHAPTER 2

COPYRIGHT AND OTHER LEGAL RIGHTS

Whether we know it or not, every creative person—writer, artist, photographer, dramatist, etc.—depends on (and really should understand) the concept of "copyright." Without copyright, creative people could not survive—at least as creators—and the world would be deprived of their creations. Happily, copyright exists, and creators—and the world—don't have to face that unthinkable alternative. But what exactly is copyright, and what should creators know about it?

COPYRIGHT BASICS

In brief, copyright refers to the legal protection that is provided to most (but not necessarily all) created works—called in the current federal Copyright Act "works of authorship." It is a kind of monopoly the law gives to creative people for their creations. As we will see below, to be protected, the work must be "fixed," that is, on paper, on computer disk, on film, on canvas, etc.—it can't be merely ephemeral or just spontaneously performed—and it must contain a minimal amount of "originality." And, as we will also see below, although the law's "protection" is extensive—it generally prevents others from copying (in whole or in part, directly or indirectly) your work—it is not absolute, the most important exception being the doctrine that allows others to make "fair use" of your work.

Where does "copyright" come from?

Copyright is a creation of law, which means it comes from the folks who write (and then interpret and implement) the laws that govern those who are subject to them. The first copyright "law" can be traced to 1710 England, but for our purposes we will start with the birth of this nation. Specifically, Article I of the U.S. Constitution, which created and granted specific powers to the new Congress, authorized Congress "to promote the Progress of Science and useful Arts, by securing for limited Times to Authors and Inventors the exclusive Right to their respective Writings and Discoveries."

Pursuant to that power, Congress enacted the first Copyright Act in 1790. Since then, there has always been a federal copyright law in the United States, with major revisions made when developments in communications rendered the existing law inapplicable or anachronistic. On January 1, 1978, the first major revision of our law in almost 70 years took general effect. The Copyright Act of 1976 was the result of more than 20 years of study, drafting, and compromise by the various (often conflicting) interests directly affected by copyright law. But it's now more than 40 years old—it was enacted at a time when words like "Internet," "software," and "websites" had little or no relevance to copyright or creators. Many believe another major overhaul is needed, and the U.S. Congress is now taking preliminary steps toward one.

What should all creators know about copyright?

This chapter will review the kinds of works that are eligible for copyright protection, the nature of the rights that copyright confers, the "fair use" doctrine and the formalities that must be complied with to secure copyright protection. It will also discuss legal protections available to creators apart from copyright. In a separate chapter, the book will discuss how our current copyright law has adapted to the cyber revolution, which happened after the current Act came into effect.

Do we "own" the copyrights in our works?

Copyright is a form of legal protection given to a wide variety of creative works, but it is also "property" that one "owns," much as one owns a car, a computer, or shares of stock. This means we can sell it (in whole or in part), or just "license" to others some or all of the rights it provides, or give it away (including in our wills)—or just keep it to ourselves, so that no one ever gets to see the work covered by the copyright. Under current law, only one kind of copyright is available to creative people for virtually all creative works: the protection afforded by the federal Copyright Act of 1976. Creative works either enjoy the protection of the Act or they have no copyright protection.

Before 1978, there were two systems of copyright available to creators. The first, known as "common law copyright," was available through state law and applied to works that had never been published or otherwise publicly disseminated. The second, the federal Copyright Act of 1909, applied mainly to published works. With the enactment of the 1976 Act, virtually all prior systems of common law copyright were abolished. In legal parlance, the new act substantially "preempted" common law copyright protection.

How does copyright protect creators?

The protection of the Copyright Act is extensive. Anyone who uses a copyrighted work in a way that constitutes an infringement may be subject to civil remedies, including an injunction, forfeiture of the infringing items or the obligation to pay the copyright owner all profits from the infringement, money damages, and the owner's attorneys' fees. In certain cases, the infringer may also be subject to criminal penalties. Further questions in this chapter deal with what constitutes infringement.

What kinds of works can be protected by copyright under the Act?

Section 102 of the Act states: "Copyright protection subsists in original works of authorship fixed in any tangible medium of expression, now known or later developed, from which they can be perceived, reproduced, or otherwise communicated, either directly or with the aid of a machine or device." There are two fundamental requirements for copyright protection: The work must be "original," and it must be "fixed" in a "tangible medium of expression."

What is the "originality" requirement?

This requirement is relatively undemanding. To be sufficiently original, a work does not have to be novel, unique, or ingenious, as a patentable invention must be. It must simply have been created or originated by an "author" rather than found or identically copied from another work, and it must present more than a trivial variation on prior works from which it is derived. Perhaps the best summation of originality was provided by Judge Learned Hand, who wrote that "if by some magic a man who had never known it were to compose anew Keats's 'Ode on a Grecian

Urn,' he would be an 'author,' and, if he copyrighted it, others might not copy that poem, though they might of course copy Keats's." To illustrate how limited the requirement of originality is, the Copyright Act states that compilations or anthologies of previously copyrighted (or public domain) works are eligible for copyright, originality being in the selection and ordering of the included works. Similarly, a collage composed of found objects is the original work of an artist who created the work through a process of selection and arrangement, and is copyrightable.

A major decision by the Supreme Court illustrates the point. The case involved a telephone company in rural Kansas that simply copied the directory of a competing company. That company sued for copyright infringement, but the Supreme Court, reversing two lower courts, dismissed the case. Emphasizing the requirement of originality, the Court said: "The distinction is one between creation and discovery: The first person to find and report a particular fact has not created the fact; he or she has just discovered its existence." Copyright protection for a compilation in which the facts speak for themselves, the Court held, is "thin" because the "only conceivable expression is the manner in which the compiler has 'selected and arranged the facts.'" The Court specifically rejected a line of lower court cases that upheld copyright protection for works that were derived from "the sweat of [the compiler's] brow," holding that "the principal focus should be on whether the selection, coordination, and arrangement are sufficiently original to merit protection." The Court found the plaintiff's directory did not have that degree of originality and thus was not entitled to copyright protection.

Every work must be evaluated on its own to determine whether it is sufficiently original. There is no one formulation or standard that articulates the requirement. The courts have found that mezzotint reproductions of eighteenth- and nineteenth-century paintings, a scale-model reproduction of Rodin's *Hands of God* sculpture, and computer answer sheets for standardized tests needed some judgment, skill, and expertise for their creation and were "original" enough for copyright.

What is required for a work to be "fixed in a tangible medium of expression"?

According to the Copyright Act, "A work is 'fixed' in a tangible medium of expression when its embodiment in a copy . . . by or under the authority of the author, is sufficiently permanent or stable to permit it to be perceived, reproduced, or otherwise communicated for a period of more than transitory duration." The statutory definition is intentionally broad so that it will be applicable to modes of expression developed in the future that are unknown today.

Preparatory works such as sketches, drafts, models, and notes, as well as finished works such as manuscripts, paintings, sculptures, motion pictures, and audio- and videotapes, satisfy the fixation requirement. But oral recitations or performances, however original and otherwise eligible for federal copyright, do not satisfy the fixation test. An unauthorized taping of an oral recitation would not be eligible for copyright because the statutory definition requires the "embodiment" to be "by or under the authority of the author." (Even though such an unfixed rendition will not qualify for federal copyright protection, it may—as is discussed later in this chapter—qualify for other forms of legal protection.)

What works are protected?

Section 102 of the Act provides a partial answer: "Works of authorship include the following categories: (1) literary works; (2) musical works, including any accompanying words; (3) dramatic works, including any accompanying music; (4) pantomimes and choreographic works; pictorial, graphic, and sculptural works; (5) motion pictures and other audiovisual works; and (6) sound recordings." Most of those terms (for example, "literary works" and "pictorial, graphic, and sculptural works") are given more specific definitions in the Act. "Literary works" are defined as "works, other than audiovisual works, expressed in words, numbers, or other verbal or numerical symbols or indicia, regardless of the nature of the material objects, such as books, periodicals, manuscripts, phonorecords, film, tape, disks, or cards, in which they are embodied."

Significantly, the six categories listed in Section 102 do not exhaust the kinds of works that may qualify for copyright protection. The introduction to the listing contains the word "include," which the Act defines as "illustrative and not limitative." Still, not every creative work qualifies for copyright protection.

WHAT'S NOT PROTECTED BY COPYRIGHT?

Unfortunately, there is no clear and concise answer. The 1976 Copyright Act provides several categories or descriptions of works that are not subject to copyright protection. But the precise meaning of the statutory language is frequently difficult to discern and is open to interpretation and debate. Section 102(b) provides: "In no case does copyright protection extend to any idea, procedure, process, system, method of operation, concept, principle, or discovery, regardless of the form in which it is described, explained, illustrated, or embodied in such work." This is a very important limitation on copyright protection.

The traditional statement of this rule is that copyright protects only the "expression" of an idea and not the idea itself. But it is often far from clear just when the non-copyrightable "idea" becomes the copyrightable "expression" of that idea. For example, in one famous case the author of the play *Abie's Irish Rose* sued the producer of the motion picture *The Cohens and the Kellys* for copyright infringement. Both works involved the marriage of a Jewish man to an Irish woman; their fathers opposed the marriage but ultimately came to bless it. The court rejected the claim of infringement, declaring:

> Upon any work, and especially upon a play, a great number of patterns of increasing generality will fit equally well, as more and more of the incident is left out. The last may perhaps be no more than the most general statement of what the play is about, and at times might consist only of its title; but there is a point in this series of abstractions where they are no longer protected, since otherwise the playwright could prevent the use of his ideas, to which, apart from their expression, his property is never extended.

Hypothetically, a novel about a boy who attends a magical school for wizards would not necessarily infringe the copyrights protecting the "Harry Potter" books, and a comic strip or motion picture about a man of extraordinary strength who can fly would not necessarily infringe the copyrights protecting "Superman." On a more prosaic level, the U.S. Copyright Office, the federal agency responsible for administering the Copyright Act, has articulated the idea-expression distinction as follows:

> Copyright protection extends to a description, explanation, or illustration of an idea or system assuming that the requirements of the copyright law are met. Copyright in such a case protects the

particular literary or pictorial form in which an author chooses to express himself. However, it gives the copyright owner no exclusive rights in the idea, plan, method, or system involved.

Suppose, for example, that an author copyrights a book explaining a new system for food processing. The copyright in the book . . . will prevent others from publishing the author's text and illustrations describing the author's ideas for machinery, processes, and merchandising methods. However, it will not give him any rights against others who adopt the ideas for commercial purposes, or who develop or use the machinery, processes, or methods described in the book.

At some point, a subsequent author's use of an author's "ideas" may well violate the copyright in the original work, because at some point the first author's combination of "ideas" becomes protectable expression for copyright purposes. Just when that point will be reached is impossible to say in general. Each case depends on its circumstances.

What about an author's research and the discovery of facts?

As noted above, facts as such are not protectable by copyright, even if they are newly discovered by an author. Copyright protects only the original creative work of an author. Discovered facts do not meet that requirement. As a recent case put it:

Obviously, a fact does not originate with the author of a book describing the fact. Neither does it originate with one who "discovers" the fact. The discoverer merely finds and records. He may not claim that the facts are "original" with him although there may be originality and hence authorship in the manner of reporting, i.e., the "expression" of the facts. . . . Thus, since facts do not owe their origin to any individual, they may not be copyrighted and are part of the public domain available to every person.

Similarly, the courts have decided that an author's research, no matter how diligent or important, cannot be copyrighted. As that recent case explained:

The valuable distinction in copyright law between facts and the expression of facts cannot be maintained if research is held to be copyrightable. There is no rational basis for distinguishing between facts and the research involved in obtaining facts. To hold that research is copyrightable is no more or no less than to hold that the facts discovered as a result of research are entitled to copyright protection.

In its decision in the telephone directory case, the Supreme Court conclusively laid to rest the notion that an author's effort in assembling facts could itself merit copyright protection. But what must be added to facts to merit protection is not always clear. One leading case involved a nonfiction book, *Who Destroyed the Hindenberg?*, in which the author presented the results of his exhaustive research and his theory of what happened to the German dirigible. When a movie was produced on the same subject propounding the same theory, the author sued for copyright infringement. Even though it was admitted that the book was used in the making of the movie, the federal court of appeals rejected the suit, holding that neither the author's research nor his theory were protected by copyright. As the court put it:

> In works devoted to historical subjects, it is our view that a second author may make significant use of prior work, so long as he does not bodily appropriate the expression of another. This principle is justified by the fundamental policy undergirding the copyright laws—the encouragement of contributions to recorded knowledge. The "financial reward guaranteed to the copyright holder is but an incident of this general objective, rather than an end in itself." . . . Knowledge is expanded as well, by granting new authors of historical works a relatively free hand to build upon the work of their predecessors.

But that case has not been uniformly followed. In a federal case in Chicago, books presenting the theory that bank robber John Dillinger was not killed by the FBI in 1934 as generally believed were held copyrightable as "historical nonfiction." In the key case, the court held that the author's interpretive story—that Dillinger did not die but lived on the West Coast for many years after the FBI killed the wrong man—was protectable by copyright even if the idea and facts used in support of the theory were not. The court held that "interpretative theories based on historical facts are copyrightable."

Thus, as the Supreme Court has acknowledged, "In the realm of factual narrative, the law is currently unsettled regarding the ways in which non-copyrightable elements combine with the author's contributions to form protected expression." This difficulty may be due in part to a recognition of the dilemma facing nonfiction writers: There may be only limited ways to express the facts. Thus a direct rendition of those facts may not entail the requisite creativity for copyright purposes. However, protection could still be available for the "association, presentation, and combination of the ideas and thought which go to make up the [author's] literary combination." So although the "ordinary" phrase may not be protected, "its use in a sequence of expressive words doesn't cause the entire passage to lose protection."

Legal protection for ideas apart from copyright is discussed later in this chapter.

What about names, titles, and short phrases?

According to the Copyright Office, "To be protected by copyright, a work must contain at least a certain minimum amount of authorship in the form of original literary, musical, or graphic expression. Names, titles, and other short phrases do not meet these requirements."

The office has provided a listing of the kinds of phrases that do not qualify for copyright. It includes "names or pseudonyms of individuals (including a pen name or stage name)," "titles of works," and "catchwords, catch phrases, mottoes, slogans, or short advertising expressions." To emphasize the point, the office states that this ineligibility "is true even if the name, title, or short phrase is novel, distinctive, or lends itself to a play on words." But here too, at some point a short phrase, perhaps even a title, will be long enough to qualify for copyright. Just how long is "long enough" is impossible to state in a single formulation. The determination whether any particular phrase or title will qualify for copyright protection requires a case-by-case evaluation.

What about works of the U.S. government?

The Copyright Act expressly provides that "copyright protection . . . is not available for any work of the United States Government," which the Act defines as "a work prepared by an officer or employee of the United States Government as a part of that person's official duties."

It should usually be fairly easy to determine whether a work fits within this exclusion. Statements and reports issued by congressional committees or federal agencies and opinions of the federal courts are clearly not eligible for copyright and may be used freely. Sometimes the determination may not be so easy. One leading case involved the copyrightability of speeches by an admiral of the U.S. Navy that were written and delivered on his own time but typed by his Navy assistant on Navy equipment and stationery on Navy time. The court ruled that the speeches did not qualify as "works of the United States Government" and thus could be copyrighted by the admiral because they were not given as a part of his official duties but as an individual. Presumably, then, a congressman's speech on the floor of the House would not be eligible for copyright but the same speech to a college audience might be. The fact that material is included in the Congressional Record does not mean anyone can use it; it may have been quoted there and created by someone other than an officer or employee of the U.S. government.

A more difficult issue is whether copyright can be secured in works prepared under a government contract or grant. The Act is deliberately silent on this point; it was Congress's intent to allow each government agency to make a determination on copyrightability for each situation. Congress anticipated that if the agency hired an outside person or firm to do the work "merely as an alternative to having one of its own employees prepare the work," then the right to copyright would not be granted. It is foreseeable, however, that many contracted works will be eligible for copyright. The matter is open to negotiation, and creators who are considering doing work under the auspices of the federal government should ensure that their work will be copyrightable.

What about works in the "public domain"?

By definition, works in the public domain are not protected by copyright and can be used—copied and reproduced—freely. But when does a work become public domain? Because the Constitution proscribes that copyright can only extend for "limited times," the most obvious answer is that a work will fall into the public domain when its "term" of copyright expires. (Copyright terms are discussed later in this chapter.) Another answer is when the work is not eligible for copyright, as discussed above. Also, a copyright owner can "dedicate" his work to the public domain. All of Shakespeare's works, for example, are in the public domain. With a few limited exceptions, once a work falls into the public domain, there is no way to return it to copyright protection.

Can characters be protected by copyright?

Definitely, if they are in pictorial form. Pictorial renditions of Mickey Mouse, Dick Tracy, Wonder Woman, and other created characters are eligible. It is more difficult for literary characters, those depicted in words but not pictorially, to meet the level of expression required for copyright protection. Some courts have held that such characters are protectable if they "constitute the story being told" rather than being just the "vehicle" for telling the story. Applying this reasoning, one court held that Dashiell Hammett's transfer to Warner Brothers of the copyright in his first "Sam Spade" story, *The Maltese Falcon*, did not transfer the copyright in the Spade character, so that Hammett was free to continue to use Spade in his work. One of the most famous judicial statements on the issue came from Judge Learned Hand in the *Abie's Irish Rose* case:

> If *Twelfth Night* were copyrighted, it is quite possible that a second comer might so closely imitate Sir Toby Belch or Malvolio as to infringe, but it would not be enough that for one of his characters he cast a riotous knight who kept wassail to the discomfort of the household, or a vain and foppish steward who became amorous of his mistress. These would be no more than Shakespeare's "ideas" in the play, as little capable of monopoly as Einstein's Doctrine of Relativity, or Darwin's theory of the Origin of Species. It follows that the less developed the characters, the less they can be copyrighted; that is the penalty an author must bear for marking them too indistinctly.

Thus, a well-delineated literary character will be protectable by copyright.

What about three-dimensional works?

Three-dimensional works, such as sculptural works, are generally copyrightable under the protection for pictorial, graphic, and sculptural works, but with one critical exception: Works that are "utilitarian" or "useful articles" are generally not copyrightable. Section 101 of the Copyright Act provides that copyrightable works "shall include works of artistic craftsmanship insofar as their form but not their mechanical or utilitarian aspects are concerned; the design of a useful article, as defined in this section, shall be considered a pictorial, graphic, or sculptural work only if, and only to the extent that, such design incorporates pictorial, graphic, or sculptural features that can be identified separately from and are capable of existing independently of, the utilitarian aspects of the article."

Courts have struggled to determine when something is utilitarian (hence not protected by copyright) and when there is additional artistic expression (thus permitting protection). An initial question is whether the separate identification and existence of the "design" must be physical or simply conceptual. Although "physical" separability was adopted by at least one court, the preferred view seems to be that "the features only need to be conceptually separable from the utilitarian functions of the garments to be entitled to protection under the copyright law." Under that view,

> a useful article will be denied protection "if the design elements reflect a merger of aesthetic and functional considerations. Conversely, where design elements can be identified as reflecting the designer's artistic judgment exercised independently of functional influences, conceptual separability exists." The test does not require that applied art be completely divorced from utilitarian concerns, but only that the artistic form not be influenced "in significant measure" by functional considerations.

The design process will be examined carefully. But too literal an application of this test may make an article's copyrightability determined by where in the creative process an artist considered functional elements. Copyrightability ultimately "should depend on the extent to which the work reflects artistic expression uninhibited by functional considerations."

In 2017, the U.S. Supreme Court had to decide whether the design on specific cheerleaders' uniforms were—or were not—copyrightable. After an exhaustive review of how various courts across the country have addressed the underlying legal issue—without reaching anything like a consensus—the federal appeals court in the case concluded that because "the graphic features of Varsity's designs can be identified separately from, and are capable of existing independently of, the utilitarian aspects of [cheerleading uniforms]," those graphic designs "are copyrightable subject matter." In an eagerly awaited decision, in March 2017 the Supreme Court held "that a feature incorporated into the design of a useful article is eligible for copyright protection only if the feature (1) can be perceived as a two- or three-dimensional work of art separate from the useful article and (2) would qualify as a protectable pictorial, graphic, or sculptural work—either on its own or fixed in some other tangible medium of expression—if it were imagined separately from the useful article into which it is incorporated." The court held that the uniform designs were copyrightable.

WHAT RIGHTS DOES COPYRIGHT CONFER?

Copyright grants its owner a form of legal monopoly over her work. It is not an absolute monopoly, however; it consists of specific "exclusive rights." The Copyright Act lists five exclusive rights that belong to a copyright owner: (1) to reproduce the copyrighted work in copies; (2) to prepare derivative works based upon the copyrighted work; (3) to distribute copies of the copyrighted work to the public by sale or other transfer of ownership, or by rental, lease, or lending; (4) in the case of literary, musical, dramatic, and choreographic works, pantomimes, and motion pictures and other audiovisual works, to perform the copyrighted work publicly; and (5) in the case of literary, musical, dramatic, and choreographic works, pantomimes, and pictorial, graphic, or sculptural works, to display the copyrighted work publicly.

Thus, the copyright grants its owner the right to control the destiny of the copyrighted work. The owner can determine whether to expose it to the public, and if it is exposed, the owner can control (at least initially) the persons and means through which the exposure will take place. Any right the copyright owner possesses can be transferred to others.

These exclusive rights do not give the copyright owner complete control. The Act provides specified limitations; for example, libraries and archives have certain rights to reproduce copyrighted works without the copyright owner's consent. In addition, the owner of an authorized copy of a copyrighted work (e.g., a book purchased in a bookstore) can do whatever he or she wishes with the copy, including reselling it, without the copyright owner's consent. This is known as the "first sale" doctrine. But probably the most significant limitation on the exclusive rights of the copyright owner is "fair use."

What is a "derivative" work?

One of the five "exclusive rights" (discussed more fully below) that copyright confers on a copyright owner is the right "to prepare derivative works based upon the copyrighted work." The Act defines a derivative work as "a work based upon one or more preexisting works, such as a translation, musical arrangement, dramatization, fictionalization, motion picture version, sound recording, art reproduction, abridgment, condensation, or any other form in which a work may be recast, transformed, or adapted." It adds that "a work consisting of editorial revisions, annotations, elaborations, or other modifications which, as a whole, represent an original work of authorship, is a 'derivative work.'"

Thus, whenever a book is translated into another language or abridged, a movie is based on a book or a play, a television series is based on a movie, or a book is based on a short story or a magazine article, the resulting works are derivative works the original copyright owner can control. Conversely, derivative works created without the consent of the copyright owner infringe the copyright in the original work.

The derivative work is entitled to a separate copyright. However, the Act states that the copyright in the derivative work "extends only to the material contributed by the author of such work, as distinguished from the preexisting material employed in the work, and does not imply any exclusive right in the preexisting material," and that it "is independent of, and does not affect or enlarge the scope, duration, ownership, or subsistence of, any copyright protection in the preexisting material." In other words, only the new matter in the derivative work is protected by its copyright.

As a result of these provisions, it is possible that a derivative work (e.g., a movie version or a translation of a book) can be protected by its own copyright even if the underlying book is no longer copyrighted. This protection is limited: others are free to create movie versions or translations of the same underlying book as long as they do not copy from a previously copyrighted movie version or translation. And the right of the owner of the copyright in a derivative work to continue to exploit that work may be limited by the terms of the underlying grant authorizing the derivative work.

What about collections of separate works, such as an almanac, an anthology, or an issue of a magazine?

The Copyright Act has provisions for "compilations" and "collective works." A compilation is "a work formed by the collection and assembling of preexisting materials or of data that are selected, coordinated, or arranged in such a way that the resulting work as a whole constitutes an original work of authorship." Furthermore, "the term 'compilation' includes collective works."

A collective work is "a work, such as a periodical issue, anthology, or encyclopedia, in which a number of contributions, constituting separate and independent works in themselves, are assembled into a collective whole." Thus, unlike derivative works (which by definition require adaptation and change of the underlying copyrighted work), a compilation or collective work presumably involves no changes to the underlying material. As with derivative works, compilations (including collective works) can have their own copyrights, but the copyrights are independent from and do not affect the existence, duration, or effectiveness of the copyright in the underlying material.

LIMITATIONS ON COPYRIGHT PROTECTION

Although the concept of "fair use" was not expressly recognized in the copyright acts before the current one, it has long been an integral part of the law as interpreted by the courts. Faced with claims of infringement that seemed unfair, unrealistic, or inconsistent with the constitutional purpose of copyright to promote knowledge, and perhaps inspired by the spirit of the First Amendment, the courts had little difficulty creating a fair use limitation on rights of copyright owners to prevent unauthorized use. Thus, a judicially created doctrine of fair use was well established in the law of copyright before the 1976 Copyright Act was enacted.

In late 2016, the influential federal court of appeals in New York issued a major opinion revisiting the parameters of contemporary fair use law. In so doing, it reiterated the philosophy underlying the fair use doctrine: "First, the law affords copyright protection to promote not simply individual interests, but—in the words of the Constitution—'the progress of science and useful arts' for the benefit of society as a whole. As the Supreme Court has explained, copyright protection is based on the 'economic philosophy… that encouragement of individual effort [for] personal gain is the best way to advance public welfare.' Second, and consistent with this public purpose, the law has long recognized that 'some opportunity for fair use of copyrighted materials' is necessary to promote progress in science and art. [As one court put it,] the fair use doctrine 'permits courts to avoid rigid application of the copyright statute when, on occasion, it would stifle the very creativity which that law is designed to foster.'"

What happened in 1976?

The Copyright Act of 1976 was the first federal copyright legislation that expressly recognized a fair use limitation on the rights of copyright owners to prevent certain uses of their works. Section 107 provided that notwithstanding the grant of exclusive rights to copyright owners, "the fair use of a copyrighted work . . . for purposes such as criticism, comment, news reporting, teaching (including multiple copies for classroom use), scholarship, or research, is not an infringement of copyright." In the congressional reports accompanying the 1976 Act, the drafters of the law provided other, more explicit examples of fair use:

> Quotations of excerpts in a review or criticism for purposes of illustration or comment; quotation of short passages in a scholarly or technical work, for illustration or clarification of the author's observations; use in a parody of some of the content of the work parodied; summary of an address or article, with brief quotations,

in a news report; reproduction by a library of a portion of a work to replace part of a damaged copy; reproduction by a teacher or student of a small part of a work to illustrate a lesson; reproduction of a work in legislative or judicial proceedings or reports; incidental and fortuitous reproduction, in a news reel or broadcast, of a work located in the scene of an event being reported.

Did Congress provide any guidance?

As with many other concepts at the heart of copyright law, it is much easier to describe fair use in general than to give it a specific definition. Indeed, it has been stated that "since the doctrine is an equitable rule of reason, no generally applicable definition is possible, and each case raising the question must be decided on its own facts."

To assist in this effort, Congress has provided in the 1976 Act four factors "to be considered" in "determining whether the use made of a work in any particular case is a fair use": "(1) the purpose and character of the use, including whether such use is of a commercial nature or is for nonprofit educational purposes; (2) the nature of the copyrighted work; (3) the amount and substantiality of the portion used in relation to the copyrighted work as a whole; and (4) the effect of the use upon the potential market for or value of the copyrighted work."

What's the most important factor?

Until fairly recently, the fourth factor—the financial impact of the use on the copyright owner—was considered the most important. But no longer. Today, the first factor is the most important. As first propounded in a 1990 law review article by a federal appeals court judge, and then endorsed by a 1994 Supreme Court decision, the fair use determination should give considerable weight to whether the new work "transforms" the original. As the 2016 appeals court decision explained: "The Supreme Court has stated that 'the goal of copyright . . . is generally furthered by the creation of transformative works.' But how does a court decide whether and to what extent the new work is 'transformative'? [The Supreme Court instructed] that a court properly considers 'whether the new work merely supersedes the objects of the original creation, or instead adds something new, with a further purpose or different character, altering the first with new expression, meaning, or message.'"

How is it determined whether a use "transforms" the original?

Every case will ultimately turn on its own facts and circumstances, and it may not be possible to know in advance how the courts will answer that question in every case. But that recent appellate decision, making a significant change from previous cases, did provide this further guidance: "The focus of inquiry is not simply on the new work, i.e., on whether that work serves a purpose or conveys an overall expression, meaning, or message different from the copyrighted material it appropriates. Rather, the critical inquiry is whether the new work uses the copyrighted material itself for a purpose, or imbues it with a character, different from that for which it was created. . . . Otherwise, any play that needed a character to sing a song, tell a joke, or recite a poem could use unaltered copyrighted material with impunity, so long as the purpose or message of the play was different from that of the appropriated material." Further, "to qualify as a fair use" in the absence of such a different purpose, the new work "generally must alter the original with 'new expression, meaning, or message.'"

Two cases, both further discussed below, provide examples. In one, the Supreme Court held that a rap parody of a popular country song was transformative, while in the other the federal appeals court in New York held in 2016 that the (unchanged) use of a famous comedy routine in a stage play was not.

This new emphasis represents a significant constriction of the kinds of uses that will be found "fair," but it remains to be seen how the courts will actually implement that new direction in future cases. For now, however, it should serve as a warning sign to creators intending to use others' copyrighted work to (at least) be aware of this new judicial approach to fair use, because a use that is not found to be fair will very likely be found to be an infringement, with potentially severe consequences.

What about the "commercial" nature of the use?

The 2016 appeals court decision also reversed course a bit on the relevance of the commercial nature of the second use. Noting that it had previously "sometimes assigned little weight to the commercial nature of a secondary use even absent a transformative purpose," the court made clear that, at least in the absence of a finding of transformation, the commercial nature of the second use must be considered as weighing against a finding of fair use.

What about the second factor?

The second factor, the nature of the copyrighted work, requires little comment. In works eligible for copyright, some obviously lend themselves far more readily than others to unauthorized use. As the Supreme Court has observed, certain "works are closer to the core of intended copyright protection than others, with the consequence that fair use is more difficult to establish when the former works are copied." The central distinction is between "creative" and "factual" works. For example, in the 2016 appellate decision the court found that the copyrighted work in question—

an original comedy sketch created for public entertainment—"lies at the heart of copyright's intended protection." Thus, while the secondary user of noncreative information can more readily claim fair use based on the law's recognition of "a greater need to disseminate factual works than works of fiction or fantasy," the secondary user of a creative work must justify the use, usually by explaining the functional or creative rationale behind its unauthorized use.

What about the third factor?

The third factor, the amount and substantiality of the portion used, generates the most questions by potential users (e.g., writers and publishers who want to include portions of the copyrighted work of others in their work). Invariably they ask: "How many words, how many pages, how many illustrations, can we use without having to get permission from the copyright owner?" There is no one answer to this question. Fair use determinations can be made only after evaluating all the factors as applied to the surrounding circumstances. Nevertheless, it is obvious that the more one takes (especially as that taking represents an increasingly significant portion of the entire copyrighted work), the less likely it is that the use will be found fair.

And quantity alone is not determinative of this factor. The quality or significance of what is taken is also relevant. For example, in the recent appellate decision, the court noted: "While the portion of the Routine copied by defendants takes less than two minutes to perform, it plainly reveals the singular joke underlying the entire Routine: that words understood by one person as a question can be understood by another as an answer. Moreover, defendants repeatedly exploit that joke through a dozen variations. This manifests substantial copying." The court also invoked earlier cases, holding that the third factor "favored plaintiffs where defendants copied approximately 300 words verbatim in light of the 'expressive value of the excerpts' and 'that copying even few words of challenged work can constitute substantial taking if it amounts to taking [the] heart of [the] original work.'" But the court also observed "even a substantial taking, however, can constitute fair use if justified, as where 'some purposes require copying entirety of copyrighted work.'" The court suggested that the "crux" of the third factor inquiry is whether "no more was taken than necessary."

And what about the fourth factor?

The final factor, once (but no longer) considered "undoubtedly the single most important element of fair use," is "the effect of the use upon the potential market for or value of the copyrighted work." Actual damage to the market does not have to be demonstrated; it is sufficient if the use has the potential to damage the market. And, as the recent appellate decision made clear, this factor is not only concerned with direct harm to the market for the original work; also relevant is "the possibility of defendants' use adversely affecting the licensing market for the [original work]." The court explained: "While derivative markets are not the principal focus of the fourth inquiry, that does not mean that they are irrelevant. . . . A court considering fair use properly identifies and weighs relevant harm to the derivative market for a copyrighted work, which market includes uses that creators of original works might 'license others to develop.' . . . [T]he impact on potential licensing revenues is a proper subject for consideration in assessing the fourth factor."

Is fair use law different when unpublished material is used?

It used to be. Prior to 1992, several court decisions held that the use of unpublished material—such as J.D. Salinger's letters in an unauthorized biography—could rarely if ever be found fair, solely because of their unpublished nature. But in that year Congress added a sentence to Section 107—the fair use provision—that largely overruled those cases. That sentence stated: "The fact that a work is unpublished shall not itself bar a finding of fair use if such finding is made upon consideration of all the above factors." And, since then, courts have found uses of unpublished works to qualify as "fair," although the courts continue to consider the original work's unpublished status in conducting their fair use analyses.

What about satire and parody?

Prior to 1994, several lower courts had held that works of parody and satire could be—and sometimes were the epitome of—fair use. But it took a unanimous decision by the Supreme Court in that year to remove any doubt. That case involved a rap group's parody of a classic Roy Orbison country song, "Oh, Pretty Woman," which "quickly degenerates into a play on words, substituting predictable lyrics with shocking ones" to show "how bland and banal the Orbison song" is. The Court declared: "Suffice it to say now that parody has an obvious claim to transformative value, as [the owner of the original song] itself does not deny. Like less ostensibly humorous forms of criticism, it can provide social benefit, by shedding light on an earlier work, and, in the process, creating a new one. We thus line up with the courts that have held that parody, like other comment or criticism, may claim fair use under [the fair use statute]."

Is there a difference between parody and satire?

In the "Oh, Pretty Woman" case, the Court defined "parody" as follows: "Parody needs to mimic an original to make its point, and so has some claim to use the creation of its victim's (or collective victims') imagination, whereas satire can stand on its own two feet and so requires justification for the very act of borrowing." And the Court, quoting from two prominent dictionaries, wrote this: "Satire has been defined as a work 'in which prevalent follies or vices are assailed with ridicule,' . . . or are 'attacked through irony, derision, or wit.'"

Although many courts both before and after the "Oh, Pretty Woman" decision have used the terms interchangeably, several courts have made this distinction: "By contrast to parody, when the original work is incidental to the alleged infringer's comment on a broader topic, the work is 'better characterized' as a satire. . . . In [one famous case], the alleged infringer, 'appropriation artist' Jeff Koons, cut out part of a fashion photograph ('Silk Sandals') depicting the legs of a model wearing sandals, and repositioned the image in a landscape of legs surrounded by abundantly glazed confections. The final product is a comment on mass imagery, consumerism, overindulgence, and desire." The court found that Koons's work was "better characterized" as a satire, rather than a parody, because "its message appears to target the genre of which 'Silk Sandals' is typical, rather than the individual photograph itself."

That court continued: "Parody is afforded more leeway than satire under the fair use doctrine because parody necessarily requires the parodist to mimic the original to make its point, while satire 'can stand on its own two feet,' and thus requires further justification for its borrowing. . . . If the alleged infringer merely uses the original to 'get attention or avoid the drudgery in working up something fresh,' the borrower's fairness claim diminishes or even vanishes, depending on the balance of the remaining factors."

Bottom line: Works of parody and satire can and often will be found to be protected by the fair use doctrine, but not necessarily, because the courts must conclude that the work in question qualifies for such treatment and that such a finding is supported by a weighing of all the fair use factors. Especially in the fair use realm, it must be emphasized that each case depends upon its own facts and the particular court's evaluation of the four fair use factors.

Can non-transformative uses be fair?

Yes. Several recent cases have made clear that although the "transformative" nature of a work goes to the heart of the first factor, and the whole fair use evaluation, works can still be found fair without meeting that requirement. In one case, a publication obtained and made available to its subscribers an unchanged recording of a business conference call. The court found the publication's conduct fair use, noting: "While a transformative use generally is more likely to qualify as fair use, 'transformative use is not absolutely necessary for a finding of fair use' . . . and indeed, some core examples of fair use can involve no transformation whatsoever." (For example, copies made for classroom use.)

And in another case, the federal appeals court in Georgia found that although a university's unauthorized use of excerpts from copyrighted textbooks in "course packs" provided to students was not transformative, the "educational" purpose of the uses supported a fair use finding under factor one. However, for the most part, it seems reasonable to conclude that, to be considered fair use, creative works that incorporate the preexisting copyrighted work of others should "transform" those previous works.

Are there any users who are not subject to the copyright laws?

The Eleventh Amendment to the Constitution bars suits in federal courts against states by citizens of that state or any other. Applying that amendment, a number of courts ruled that claims of copyright infringement against states and their instrumentalities (most significantly, their boards of education or regents groups) could not be brought in federal court. And because the only permissible forum for copyright claims is federal court, preventing a copyright owner from suing a state in federal court effectively prevents the suit from being brought. Although these courts have generally acknowledged the injustice of this result, they have felt bound by Supreme Court precedents involving federal statutes similar to the Copyright Act. They have also invited Congress to correct the situation.

In 1990 Congress did just that. It passed a law providing that, with respect to violations of the Copyright Act occurring on or after June 26, 1990, the states and their instrumentalities, officers, and employees were not immune under the Eleventh Amendment from suits for copyright infringement and that a copyright owner has all of the same rights against the states as she would have against a private person, including the right to seek injunctions, actual and/or statutory damages, and costs and attorneys' fees.

COPYRIGHT OWNERSHIP

With two exceptions, discussed below, the Act provides that "copyright in a work vests initially in the author or authors of the work." Although the Act does not separately define the term "author," it does refer to "works of authorship," which were discussed above. Thus the person who originally creates a work of authorship—the writer of an article or a book, the painter of a painting, the sculptor of a sculpture—owns the copyright in that work. (In this book, the term "creator" includes "author.")

The current Copyright Act changed the prior law so that copyright protection now attaches to a work automatically upon its creation. Before, an unpublished work was protected if it qualified under the common-law copyright principles of the states, with federal copyright protection in the main available only after the work was published.

What are the two exceptions to the author's ownership of the copyright?

The first exception, works of the U.S. government, was discussed above. Under the Act, such works are not entitled to copyright protection. The second (and very important) exception is "works made for hire."

What is a "work made for hire," and who owns the copyright?

The Copyright Act describes two kinds of works made for hire. The first is "a work prepared by an employee within the scope of his or her employment." The works of authors and artists who are employed by newspapers, magazine or book publishers, advertising agencies, TV or motion-picture producers, or any other employer are works made for hire if they are created in the course of employment (essentially, as a part of the job). In 1989 the Supreme Court clarified how to determine whether an author or artist is such an "employee."

Some lower courts limited work-for-hire status to situations where the author or artist was a full-time salaried employee. Other lower courts concluded that the hiring party's right to control the manner and means by which the work was created was the conclusive test, regardless of the nature of the creator's employment relationship.

The Supreme Court rejected both views, particularly the requirement that the creator be a full-time salaried employee. The

Court held that the "right-to-control" factor "was but one of a host of factors to be considered in determining whether the creator of a work was an employee, none of which alone is determinative":

> Among the other factors relevant to this inquiry are the skill required; the source of the instrumentalities and tools; the location of the work; the duration of the relationship between the parties; whether the hiring party has the right to assign additional projects to the hired party; the extent of the hired party's discretion over when and how long to work; the method of payment; the hired party's role in hiring and paying assistants; whether the work is part of the regular business of the hiring party; whether the hiring party is in business; the provision of employee benefits; and the tax treatment of the hired party.

So where a freelance artist was commissioned to create art for an advertisement, the work was done at the artist's own studio, the ad was one project and not an ongoing series of different projects, the commissioning party had no right to assign the artist any additional work or determine when it would be done or by which assistants, and the payment and tax treatment was as an independent contractor, a court had no trouble finding that the work in question was not work for hire. However, if some of the work was done in the commissioning party's offices, there was a more regular relationship, or the artist received a regular salary, then the question can still be rather muddy.

The second kind of work for hire is defined as "work specially ordered or commissioned for use as a contribution to a collective work, as part of a motion picture or other audiovisual work, as a translation, as a supplementary work, as a compilation, as an instructional text, as a test, as answer material for a test, or as an atlas, if the parties expressly agree in a written instrument signed by them that the work shall be considered a work made for hire." "Supplementary work" is defined as "a work prepared for publication as a secondary adjunct to a work by another author for the purpose of introducing, concluding, illustrating, explaining, revising, commenting upon, or assisting in the use of the other work, such as forewords, afterwords, pictorial illustrations, maps, charts, tables, editorial notes, musical arrangements, answer material for tests, bibliographies, appendices, and indexes." An "instructional text" is a "literary, pictorial, or graphic work prepared for publication with the purpose of use in systematic instructional activities."

This second kind of work for hire has three significant aspects. First, works for hire are limited to the kinds set forth in the definition. Full-length books (other than instructional texts), plays, motion pictures, musical compositions, and almost all kinds of works of visual art (except illustrations for another work) can never be works for hire, which most often are articles or chapters for inclusion in magazines or books, illustrations for magazines or books, translations, or secondary contributions to a longer work, as described in the definition.

Second, the work has to be "specially ordered or commissioned." It will usually be clear that this requirement has been satisfied, but sometimes an evaluation of the surrounding circumstances will be necessary. As a leading copyright scholar put it, "The key factor would appear to be whether the motivating factor in producing the work was the [person requesting preparation of the work] who induced [its] creation."

Third, the for-hire status must be confirmed in writing by the creator and employer. The Act does not state whether the writing must be signed before the work is created. At this point, several federal courts—including in California and Illinois—have held that the writing must precede the creation, while others—including in New York—have held that the writing can be entered into after creation if it confirms a pre-creation agreement, either implicit or explicit. If the intention of the parties is to create a work-for-hire relationship, prudence suggests that the writing be signed when the work is first commissioned. It is also best for the parties to state expressly that the work "shall be considered a work for hire." Certain publishers and other parties that commission work require creators to sign blanket work-for-hire agreements, acknowledging that all work prepared by the creator for that party is work for hire; indeed, some have made signing such agreements a precondition to being assigned any work by that party. To date, the legal effectiveness of such agreements has not been established, but creators should avoid them if at all possible.

The owner of the copyright in a work made for hire is the employer, not the creator. The creator has only the rights that may be contained in the commissioning contract between the parties.

What happens when a work has two or more authors?

Under the Act, "the authors of a joint work are co-owners of copyright in the work." A "joint work" is defined as "a work prepared by two or more authors with the intention that their contributions be merged into inseparable or interdependent parts of a unitary whole." Co-owners are equal owners unless a contract between them says otherwise.

In one leading case, the federal appeals court in New York declared:

[T]he determination of whether to recognize joint authorship in a particular case requires a sensitive accommodation of competing demands advanced by at least two persons, both of whom have normally contributed in some way to the creation of a work of value. Care must be taken to ensure that true collaborators in the creative process are accorded the perquisites of co-authorship and to guard against the risk that a sole author is denied exclusive authorship status simply because another person rendered some form of assistance. Copyright law best serves the interests of creativity when it carefully draws the bounds of "joint authorship" so as to protect the legitimate claims of both sole authors and co-authors.

Addressing the Copyright Act's definition of "joint work" (quoted above), the court declared:

Some aspects of the statutory definition of joint authorship are fairly straightforward. Parts of a unitary whole are "inseparable" when they have little or no independent meaning standing alone. That would often be true of a work of written text, such as the play that is the subject of the pending litigation. By contrast, parts of a unitary whole are "interdependent" when they have some meaning standing alone but achieve their primary significance because of their combined effect, as in the case of the words and music of a song.

Then, with respect to the word "intent" in the definition, the court said:

> [I]t is hard to imagine activity that would constitute meaningful "collaboration" unaccompanied by the requisite intent on the part of both participants that their contributions be merged into a unitary whole, and the case law has read the statutory language literally so that the intent requirement applies to all works of joint authorship.

Next, the court answered in the affirmative what it called the "troublesome" question of whether the contributions of all joint authors had to be separately "copyrightable":

> The insistence on copyrightable contributions by all putative joint authors might serve to prevent some spurious claims by those who might otherwise try to share the fruits of the efforts of a sole author of a copyrightable work. . . . More important, [this] view strikes an appropriate balance in the domains of both copyright and contract law. In the absence of contract, the copyright remains with the one or more persons who created copyrightable material. Contract law enables a person to hire another to create a copyrightable work, and the copyright law will recognize the employer as "author."

Similarly, the person with non-copyrightable material who proposes to join forces with a skilled writer to produce a copyrightable work is free to make a contract to disclose his or her material in return for assignment of part ownership of the resulting copyright. . . . It seems more consistent with the spirit of copyright law to oblige all joint authors to make copyrightable contributions, leaving those with non-copyrightable contributions to protect their rights through contract.

Finally, the court addressed the situation where an editor "makes numerous useful revisions to the first draft" and where research assistants contribute to the final work:

What distinguishes the writer-editor relationship and the writer-researcher relationship from the true joint author relationship is the lack of intent of both participants in the venture to regard themselves as joint authors. Focusing on whether the putative joint authors regarded themselves as joint authors is especially important in circumstances, such as in the instant case, where one person . . . is indisputably the dominant author of the work and the only issue is whether that person is the sole author or she and another . . . are joint authors. [The trial judge] properly insisted that [the two parties] entertain in their minds the concept of joint authorship, whether or not they understood precisely the legal consequences of that relationship. . . . In many instances, a useful test will be whether in the absence of contractual agreements concerning listed

authorship, each participant intended that all would
be identified as co-authors.

Joint ownership of a work is discussed further in Chapter 5.

Can a non-joint contributor own a separate copyright in her contribution?

No. In a closely watched case in 2015, an actress who had a small
part in an independent movie claimed a separate copyright in her
performance. The full federal appeals court in California rejected
the claim, declaring: "[The actress's] theory of copyright law
would result in the legal morass we warned against in [an earlier
case]—splintering a movie into many different 'works,' even
in the absence of an independent fixation. Simply put, as [the
defendant] claimed, it 'make[s] Swiss cheese of copyrights.' . . .
Untangling the complex, difficult-to-access, and often phantom
chain of title to tens, hundreds, or even thousands of standalone
copyrights is a task that could tie the distribution chain in knots.
And filming group scenes like a public parade, or the 1963 March
on Washington, would pose a huge burden if each of the thousands
of marchers could claim an independent copyright."

And in a 2015 case in New York, the federal appeals
court rejected a claim by a film's director that he—and not
the producer—was the copyright owner of the film. (It was
undisputed that the film was not a joint work.) The court declared
that the entire film was the single "work of authorship" entitled
to copyright and that "the Copyright Act's terms, structure, and
history support the conclusion that [the director's] contributions
to the film do not themselves constitute a 'work of authorship'
amenable to copyright protection." The court added:

Filmmaking is a collaborative process typically involving artistic contributions from large numbers of people, including—in addition to producers, directors, and screenwriters—actors, designers, cinematographers, camera operators, and a host of skilled technical contributors. If copyright subsisted separately in each of their contributions to the completed film, the copyright in the film itself, which is recognized by statute as a work of authorship, could be undermined by any number of individual claims.

What can a copyright owner do with his copyright?

Pretty much anything the owner wants to. A copyright is a form of property. Like other property, it can be sold, mortgaged, leased, licensed, bequeathed by will, or given away.

The current Copyright Act allows the rights that make up the copyright to be sold separately. (Under the previous federal copyright law, separate rights emanating from the copyright could be "licensed," but the copyright itself was deemed "indivisible" and could be owned by only one party at a time.) Now, the owner of the copyright in a novel can sell (or otherwise transfer) the exclusive right to publish it in book form to one or more publishers, sell (or otherwise transfer) the right to base a movie on it to somebody else, and retain all other rights. When one exclusive right is transferred by the copyright owner, the recipient owns the right for all purposes, including the right to bring suit for infringement.

When a copyright owner wishes to sell (or otherwise transfer) one or more of the exclusive rights in the copyright, the Act provides that there must be "an instrument of conveyance, or a note or memorandum of the transfer in writing and signed by the owner of the rights conveyed or such owner's duly authorized agent." Thus an attempted oral grant of exclusive rights was held invalid as a matter of law. The transfer of a nonexclusive right, however, does not have to be in writing to be valid.

Does ownership of the physical work carry with it ownership of its copyright?

No. It used to be presumed that ownership of a work of art included the right to reproduce it and own all other rights in the work. But that presumption was changed by statute in some states, and it was eliminated in the 1976 Copyright Act, which provides (1) that "transfer of ownership of any material object," including the original of a work of art, "does not of itself convey any rights in the copyrighted work embodied in the object," and (2) conversely, that "transfer of ownership of a copyright or of any exclusive rights under a copyright" does not "convey property rights in any material object."

A significant exception involves the exclusive right "to display the copyrighted work [of visual art] publicly." The sale of the physical work does not automatically carry with it the copyright in the work, which the artist retains, but it does transfer the "display" part of the copyright.

What is the duration of copyright protection?

Determining how long copyright protection lasts is not simple. It depends on whether the work was protected by federal statutory copyright before January 1, 1978, whether it is a work for hire, and whether it is an "anonymous" or "pseudonymous" work.

Except for works for hire and anonymous or pseudonymous works, the copyright term in works that were not published by

January 1, 1978, or were created after that date, lasts for the life of the author plus 70 years. In the case of joint authors, this means 70 years after the death of the last surviving author. Anonymous or pseudonymous works and works made for hire keep their copyright for 95 years from the year of first publication or 120 years from the year of creation, whichever comes first.

For works that were protected by federal statutory copyright before January 1, 1978, (which includes all works published with copyright before then), the term is different. The prior copyright law provided for two 28-year terms, generally beginning on the date of publication.

Failure to renew for the second (renewal) term would cause the work to fall into the public domain. The 1976 Act made two changes for such works. First, the second term was extended to 47 years, making the total term 75 years. Second, the old law required renewal within the exact last year (i.e., between the 27th and 28th anniversaries of the initial publication date). The 1976 Act extended the first term to the end of the calendar year during which it would otherwise have expired. The outside renewal date is thus the December 31 after the old date. If renewal was not effected by that date, the work fell into the public domain.

Can a creator ever regain rights previously granted?

Recognizing that copyright owners may often make improvident grants of rights at a time when they have scant bargaining power and little awareness of the potential value of their work, Congress created in the 1976 Act a mechanism that enables owners (or their heirs) to "recapture" those rights.

The 1976 Act grants the copyright owner (or a specified list of beneficiaries) the right to terminate prior transfers at certain times and under certain circumstances. Its provisions are too complicated to be fully described here; instead, we will summarize some of the most important elements.

There are different termination provisions for transfers before and transfers after January 1, 1978 (the day the 1976 Act took effect):

> With respect to transfers (the term includes sales of the entire copyright as well as exclusive and nonexclusive licenses of selected rights) by an individual author-copyright owner that were made before January 1, 1978, when the two-term system was in effect, the new Act, in the words of Barbara Ringer, the register of copyrights when the Act took effect, permits an author (or certain heirs of a dead author) to reclaim rights under a copyright after the copyright has run 56 years. Since the new law extends the length of subsisting copyrights from the 56-year maximum provided in the 1909 Act to a new maximum of 75 years, the potential period covered by these terminations will usually be 19 years.

However, for those copyrights that have already been given interim extensions beyond the 56-year maximum (under nine Acts of Congress between 1962 and 1974), the years remaining to be covered by a possible termination will be fewer than nineteen, and in some cases as few as five.

For transfers made after January 1, 1978, the 1976 Act establishes a system under which the author (or certain members of a dead author's family) can terminate the grant of rights and reclaim the copyright after a specified period. Generally the minimum period will be 35 years from the date the grant was executed, but it can be longer (up to 40 years) in certain cases involving publishing rights. Exercise of this right is optional and is subject to a number of conditions and qualifications. However, the right cannot be assigned away or waived in advance; the statute says: "Termination of the grant may be effected notwithstanding any agreement to the contrary, including an agreement to make a will or to make any future grant."

Finally, terminations of transfers made before and after 1978 are subject to a complex assortment of conditions, time limits, and procedural requirements but, assuming these are met, the right to terminate will exist regardless of any contrary agreements.

COPYRIGHT FORMALITIES

Are there legal formalities that must be complied with to obtain and maintain copyright protection?

No, and yes. Upon creation of a work, nothing need be done to secure copyright protection, which is automatic. However, particularly for works that are of U.S. origin, the Act contains requirements that must be complied with if and when a work is published and an owner wants to be able to sue for infringement. These formalities relate to notice, registration and deposit, and recordation.

What are the notice requirements of the Copyright Act?

The Act previously provided that "whenever a work is published in the United States or elsewhere by authority of the copyright owner, a notice of copyright shall be placed on all publicly distributed copies from which the work can be visually perceived, either directly or with the aid of a machine or device." Publication, for these purposes, means "the distribution of copies of a work to the public by sale or other transfer of ownership, or by rental, lease, or lending."

However, this notice requirement has always been a peculiar aspect of U.S. copyright law and is not part of the law of most countries. Thus, when in 1989 the United States joined the Berne Convention (the world's largest international copyright treaty, which prohibits any formalities as a requirement of copyright protection), certain changes were made to this country's Copyright Act. After March 1, 1989 (the effective date of the Berne Convention Implementation Act), the failure to place a copyright notice on copies will not result in loss of copyright protection.

Official U.S. policy, however, is to encourage the voluntary placement of notice on copies, with the incentive that the defense of "innocent infringement," which is available to reduce potential damages if the infringer can prove he wasn't aware that the work was protected by copyright, would be unavailable to infringers of works published with proper notices.

A proper notice of copyright consists of the symbol © (the letter C in a circle), or the word "Copyright," or the abbreviation "Copr."; and the year of first publication of the work; in the case of compilations or derivative works incorporating previously published material, the year of first publication of the compilation or derivative work is sufficient. The year may be omitted where a pictorial, graphic, or sculptural work, with the accompanying text matter, if any, is reproduced in or on greeting cards, postcards, stationery, jewelry, dolls, toys, or any useful articles; and the name of the owner of copyright in the work, or an abbreviation by which the name can be recognized, or a generally known alternative designation of the owner.

The Act provides that the notice "shall be affixed to the copies in such manner and location as to give reasonable notice of the claim of copyright." (The 1909 Copyright Act required that the notice appear at specified places on a work.) The Copyright Office has issued regulations that set forth permissible kinds of notice, but the Act makes clear that other means of notice may be sufficient. The office has also declared that the notice should be permanently legible to an ordinary user of the work and not concealed from view upon reasonable examination.

What happens if notice is omitted or in error?

Now, except for the loss of protection for "innocent infringers," nothing. Moreover, the consequences of improper or omitted notice under the 1976 Act were never as severe as under the 1909 law, where omission of notice caused the work to go into the public domain. For works publicly distributed before March 1, 1989, the Act provides that if notice was omitted from "no more than a relatively small number of copies distributed to the public" or the notice contained certain errors, the copyright owner can preserve the copyright by taking certain steps spelled out in the Act, including (1) registering the work with the Copyright Office within five years of the publication without notice and (2) attempting to correct the missing or erroneous notice. For works publicly distributed after that date, the only consequence of failing to place proper notice will be the possible use of the defense of innocent infringement.

What are the notice requirements for a contribution to a magazine?

Subject to the changes discussed above in connection with works published after March 1, 1989, a contribution to a magazine may (but is not required to) bear its own notice of copyright. If the contribution does not contain its own notice, the Act provides that an overall notice for the entire work "is sufficient to satisfy the [notice] requirements . . . with respect to the separate contributions it contains regardless of the ownership of copyright in the contributions and whether or not they have been previously published." The only exception to this rule is for advertisements placed by anyone other than the publisher, which must contain their own notice. Moreover, the single notice does not affect the copyright in that contribution, which (unless the contribution is a work made for hire or an agreement provides otherwise) will be owned by the creator and not the publisher whose name almost always appears in the single notice. The Act also makes clear that "in the absence of an express transfer of the copyright or of any rights under it, the owner of copyright in the collective work is presumed to have acquired only the privilege of reproducing and distributing the contribution as part of that particular collective work, any revision of that collective work, and any later collective work in the same series."

What does registration involve?

Registration means the filing of a prescribed form with the Copyright Office together with, in most cases, one or two copies of the work and the payment of the prescribed fee. (Generally, unpublished works require one copy; published works require two.) If the Copyright Office determines that the work is eligible for copyright, it issues a certificate of copyright to the copyright owner. Published and unpublished works may be registered. The Copyright Office will upon request furnish copies of its numerous circulars on the Act and its procedures as well as copyright application forms; the office will also answer telephone inquiries: Information and Publications Section Copyright Office, Library of Congress, Washington, DC 20559, (202) 707-3000.

Registration is not required for copyright, but it is required before an infringement lawsuit involving "a work of U.S. origin" can be commenced. (In some federal jurisdictions, just an application for registration will allow a case to be filed, but complete registrations are needed in others.)

A work is of U.S. origin if it is published first in the United States, is simultaneously published in the United States and in either a Berne or non-Berne state, is an unpublished work whose authors are all U.S. nationals, or is an audiovisual work whose authors are all legal entities headquartered in the United States. A pictorial, graphic, or sculptural work incorporated in a permanent structure located in the United States and a work that is published first in a non-Berne state whose authors are all U.S. nationals are also works of U.S. origin.

Even if registration is not required, there are specific inducements to early registration for both works of U.S. origin and Berne works. Timely registration creates a rebuttable presumption that the facts stated in the certificate of registration are true and that the copyright is valid. And although registration may take place after the infringement, the copyright owner will not be entitled to an award of statutory damages or attorneys' fees in the infringement suit. (Under any circumstances, registration is required for recovery of statutory damages or attorneys' fees for infringement of a work originating in a Berne state.) If a copyright owner contemplates the possibility of an infringement action, it is important that the work be registered as early as possible.

How does one know what form to use?

The forms issued by the Copyright Office do not correspond to the enumeration of "works of authorship" set forth in the Copyright Act but relate generally to the nature of the work. Form TX is used for all kinds of printed textual material, Form VA for works of visual art, Form PA for works of the performing arts, and Form SR for sound recordings. Renewals use Form RE, and supplementary and correcting information is registered with Form CA. Some works fit into more than one category; the owner should choose the one that best applies (there are no penalties for using the wrong form). When the form is completed, it is sent, along with the necessary deposit and payment, to the Copyright Office. Most filings with the Copyright Office can easily be accomplished online.

Must a copy of a work of visual art be deposited?

No. The Act authorizes the Copyright Office to issue regulations pursuant to which "identifying material" may be deposited in lieu of a copy of the work. The office's regulations state that it will accept "photographic prints, transparencies, photostats, drawings or similar two dimensional reproductions or renderings of the work, in a form visually perceivable without the aid of a machine or device." For pictorial or graphic works, "such material shall reproduce the actual colors employed in the work," but for all other works, the material may be in black and white. Except for holograms, only one set of complete identifying material is required. A set of complete identifying material consists of "as many pieces of identifying material as are necessary to show clearly the copyrightable content of the work for which deposit is made or for which registration is sought." All the pieces of identifying material in a set must be of uniform size. Transparencies must be at least 35mm, and if they are less than 3" x 3", they must be fixed on cardboard, plastic, or similar mounts to facilitate identification and storage. Identifying material other than transparencies should be not less than 3" x 3" and not more than 9" x 12". The Copyright Office expresses a preference for 8" x 10". At least one piece of the set must indicate the title and dimensions of the work on the frame, back, mount, or elsewhere. If the work has been published with a notice of copyright, the notice and its position on the work must be shown clearly on at least one piece of identifying material. If the size or position of the notice makes it necessary, a separate drawing or similar reproduction may be submitted.

What is recordation?

Recordation is the filing—recording—of certain documents with the Copyright Office. It is not a condition of copyright protection, but it is a prerequisite to bringing a suit for infringement. As the Act puts it, "Any transfer of copyright ownership or other document pertaining to a copyright may be recorded in the Copyright Office if the document . . . bears the actual signature of the person who executed it, or if it is accompanied by a sworn or official certification that it is a true copy of the original, signed document." Recordation provides "constructive notice" of the facts stated in the document and will establish priority between conflicting transfers. The only document that the law requires to be recorded is a notice of termination of a previous transfer, which must "be recorded in the Copyright Office before the effective date of termination, as a condition to its taking effect."

What are the consequences of the United States joining the Berne Convention (other than the changes in notice and registration requirements discussed above)?

Effective on March 1, 1989, the United States joined the largest (79 members), oldest (first formalized in 1886), and most important multilateral international copyright treaty, the Berne Convention for the Protection of Literary and Artistic Works. The United States had for years been a member of the Universal

Copyright Convention, a separate and somewhat overlapping copyright treaty whose protections were not as great as those of the Berne Convention.

Membership in Berne means that the United States will be able to participate in the formulation of international copyright policy. Because Berne has increasingly become the focal point for the discussion and development of international policy relating to new technologies and the cross-border exploitation of copyrighted works, this is of potentially great value. By joining Berne, the United States established copyright relations with 24 countries where copyright relations did not exist previously. Protection under Berne is based on "national treatment": each member state has to provide to nationals of other member nations the same level of copyright protection it gives to its own citizens. A creator's rights are automatic and may not be subject to any required formalities (which is why the notice and deposit requirements of the U.S. law had to be modified). The law of the country in which protection is sought will govern, so that a copyright owner might be able to recover there for acts that would not constitute infringement in the country in which the work originated. The benefit of U.S. membership in Berne will be greatest for those whose works are widely circulated in foreign countries.

INFRINGEMENT

What constitutes infringement?

As defined by the Act, "Anyone who violates any of the exclusive rights of the copyright owner" (subject to the doctrine of fair use and the other express limitations on those rights contained in the Act) "is an infringer of the copyright." The Act does not further define what constitutes such a violation. Plainly, a copyrighted work would be infringed by reproducing it in whole or in any substantial part and by duplicating it exactly or by simulation. It is also clear that adapting a copyrighted work into a different medium (e.g., basing a movie on a novel) will also constitute infringement. However, as indicated above in the discussion of the "originality" needed for copyright protection, similarity is not enough to establish infringement. As a leading copyright authority has put it: "The rights of a copyright owner are not infringed if a subsequent work, although substantially similar, has been independently created without reference to the prior work." Thus, absent copying, there can be no infringement of copyright regardless of the extent of similarity.

It is not always easy to prove copying, but it can be established by circumstantial evidence. Thus, if the plaintiff (owner) can show that the defendant (alleged infringer) had access to the copyrighted work and that there are substantial similarities between the two works, a finding of infringement could follow. But if the defendant can prove that she actually copied from a different work or that the parts copied from the plaintiff are not copyrightable, there can be no infringement. The copying need not be verbatim. "As long as the defendant's work is substantially similar to that of the plaintiffs, and is the product of copying rather than independent effort, it will constitute an infringement of the plaintiffs 'expression.' Similarity which is not 'substantial,' even if due to copying, is a non-infringing use of the plaintiff's 'ideas.'"

What should a copyright owner do upon discovering an infringement?

First, try to stop it. Sometimes the infringement is innocent: For one reason or another, the infringer is not aware that his use constitutes an infringement. In many cases the infringer will readily agree to stop, and perhaps to make amends. Innocence is no defense to an infringement action, but it will probably affect the nature and extent of the recovery obtained by the copyright owner.

However, the owner will often conclude that a lawsuit must be brought. Indeed, it is the availability of such a suit that gives copyright protection its "teeth" and makes copyright a respected and valuable right.

What remedies are available to a copyright owner in an infringement action?

Under the Act, a copyright owner can secure an injunction against continuation of the infringement, including in appropriate cases a "preliminary injunction" before the case goes to trial; the impoundment and destruction of the infringing items, an award of the owner's damages and the infringer's profits, or an award of "statutory damages"; and in the discretion of the court, an award of the owner's attorneys' fees.

Regarding actual damages and the infringer's profits, the Act provides:

> The copyright owner is entitled to recover the actual damages suffered by him or her as a result of the infringement, and any profits of the infringer that are attributable to the infringement and are not taken into account in computing the actual damages. In establishing the infringer's profits, the copyright owner is required to present proof only of the infringer's gross revenue, and the infringer is required to prove his or her deductible expenses and the elements of profit attributable to factors other than the copyrighted work.

It is often difficult for a copyright owner to prove actual damages and/or profits realized from the infringement. Recognizing this, Congress (in both the 1909 Copyright Act and the current one) allowed the owner to elect instead an award of "statutory damages." As the Act puts it,

> The copyright owner may elect, at any time before final judgment is rendered, to recover, instead of actual damages and profits, an award of statutory damages for all infringements involved in the action, with respect to any one work, for which any one infringer is liable individually, or for which any two or more infringers are liable jointly and severally, in a sum of not less than $750 or more than $30,000 as the court considers just.

Although a finding of copyright infringement can in certain cases result in an injunction stopping the infringing use, that is not always the case. For example, where a copyrighted photograph was used in a book without permission, no injunction was granted because the court concluded that the burden on the defendant in lost sales would far outweigh the damage to the plaintiff from the use, especially since the plaintiff did not have a competing book.

The Act also provides that if the infringement was committed "willfully," the maximum statutory damages can be $150,000, and if the infringement was innocent (i.e., "the infringer was not aware and had no reason to believe that his or her acts constituted an infringement of copyright"), the minimum award of statutory damages can be $200. The Act also provides that the court may grant to the copyright owner an award of her costs of litigation, including attorneys' fees. However, it is important to remember that statutory damages and attorneys' fees will not be available unless the copyright owner complies with the registration provisions and had registered the work before the infringement began. Finally, under certain circumstances, including willful infringement "for purposes of commercial advantage or private financial gain," the infringer may also be subject to criminal penalties.

CREATORS' RIGHTS APART FROM COPYRIGHT

Are there rights protecting the work of creators other than those stemming from the Copyright Act?

Yes. The Copyright Act of 1976 preempts all other copyright protection for works that meet its requirements. Thus an original work of authorship that is fixed in a tangible medium of expression will either have copyright protection under the federal Copyright Act or none at all. But what about original works of authorship that are not so fixed, such as a recited poem or story, an improvised performance of a skit or play or dance, or an oral description of a visual design or work of art? Since these works are not eligible for protection under the Copyright Act, it seems likely that they are still protected from infringement under state common-law copyright or other similar provisions. For example, oral statements (in the context of an interview or otherwise) would not be protected by federal copyright law; to date, no court has addressed whether such statements are protected by state "common law copyright."

Similarly, rights that are not the legal equivalent of copyright may be protected by state and other federal laws. When Bette Midler sued Ford Motor Company for using a "sound-alike" in a TV commercial (i.e., the commercial used someone who sounded like Ms. Midler singing a song similar to one which she made famous), the claim was held not preempted by the Copyright

Act. The court found that California's common law protected the distinctive elements of a person's identity and that such factors, not those inherent in copyright, were the real basis for the claim. However, in 2016 the federal appeals court in St. Louis found that a professional football player's "right of publicity" claim based on the showing of films that included his play in games was "preempted" by the Copyright Act.

There are also certain rights long recognized in other countries that are frequently invoked in the United States, including in particular the rights of *droit de suite* and *droit moral*.

What is *droit de suite*?

Droit de suite has been loosely translated as the "art-proceeds" right. It is based on the belief that many artists—especially at the beginning of their careers—will sell their work at prices reflecting their then essentially nonexistent "market value," only to find over time that the "value" of their work increased dramatically. The supporters of *droit de suite* believe the artist, along with the fortunate purchaser, should share in the increase in the value of the work. *Droit de suite* gives the artist the right to receive additional payment each time a work is sold, especially if the work is resold at a price higher than at the original sale. It is recognized in a number of European countries, with differences in the kinds of sales covered (auction, dealer, private), the percentage of resale price to be paid to the artist, the length of time the right remains in effect, and whether the resale price must exceed the original price. *Droit de suite* has received some (limited) acceptance in this country.

To what extent has *droit de suite* been recognized in the United States?

In 1977 California became the first (and only) state to enact a statute giving artists the right to receive royalties on the resale of their works. The statute applies to sales of original paintings, sculptures, and drawings (but not lithographs or prints) that take place during the artist's lifetime or within 20 years of the artist's death in California or in which the seller is a California resident. The artist or his heirs receive 5 percent of the proceeds, and dealers and agents are required to withhold that percentage from the purchase price and attempt to locate and pay the artist. If the artist cannot be found, the money goes to a state art fund. The statute does not apply to the initial sale, a resale within twenty years after the artist's death, or a resale where the gross price is less than the price paid by the seller or is less than $1,000.

However, in 2016—some 43 years after the statute was enacted—a federal trial judge effectively struck down major parts of the law, holding that it was preempted by the "first sale" provision of the Copyright Act, which provides that the original (authorized) purchaser of a copy of a copyrighted work is entirely free to sell or otherwise dispose of that copy as she wishes, without any involvement by the copyright owner. That decision, which even the court rendering it called a "close" question, is now on appeal to the federal appeals court in California, and the fate of any *droit de suite* law in the United States will likely depend on how that court, and perhaps the Supreme Court, resolves the preemption issue.

It has been suggested that instead of adopting a law like California's *droit de suite* statute, states should tax the sale of art, with proceeds going to a central fund from which payments would be made to needy professional artists. Such tax funds would assist artists, would be deductible from the purchaser's other taxes, and if the rate was small, would not materially interfere with the art market. But so far this idea has not been adopted by any state.

What is *droit moral*?

Droit moral (literally, "moral right") refers to the artist's right to maintain the integrity of a work even after it has been sold. This principle has long been a cornerstone of artists' (and authors') protection in many European countries. This right is "perpetual, inalienable, and cannot be waived," and it has been further described as "non-property attributes of an intellectual and moral character which exist between a literary or artistic work and its author's personality; it is intended to protect his personality as well as his work."

Droit moral is distinct from copyright. Copyright protects the artist's right to exploit a work—it protects an artist's property right. *Droit moral* is a personal right, protecting an artist's expression: "[An artist] does more than bring into the world a unique object having only exploitive possibilities; he projects onto the work part of his personality and subjects it to the ravages of public use. There are possibilities of injury to the creator other than mere economic ones."

There are four major components of *droit moral*: integrity, paternity, divulgation, and withdrawal. The right of integrity assumes that the work of art is an expression of the artist's personality and that distortion, dismemberment, or misrepresentation of the work can adversely affect the artist's identity, personality, and honor. In a celebrated case in France, the court ruled that the artist's *droit moral* prevented the owner of a refrigerator that had been decorated by Bernard Buffet from taking the refrigerator apart and selling its six panels separately.

The right of paternity gives the artist the right to insist that his or her name be associated with the work. In France, the right cannot be waived, even by the artist. In one case where a painter had agreed to use a pseudonym in a contract commissioning works over a period of ten years, the court ruled that the artist could not be prohibited from using his real name in connection with the sale of the works.

The right of divulgation gives the artist the absolute right to determine whether and when a work is complete and ready to be shown to the public. Similar to the right of divulgation is the right to control the creation of a work. Thus, when Rosa Bonheur refused to paint a canvas pursuant to a contract, she was held liable for damages, but the court refused to order her to paint it.

Finally, the right of withdrawal gives the artist the exclusive right to withdraw a work from publication and subsequently to change the work.

Has *droit moral* been adopted in the United States?

Until recently, the United States has not been receptive to this right. When it has been asserted, the courts have noted that it has not generally been recognized in the United States and have suggested that if creators want its benefits, they should seek to secure them in contracts. But times are changing. Creative (and at times persuasive) arguments have been fashioned from other legal doctrines to secure for authors and artists some of the elements of *droit moral*. For example, although the right of divulgation has not specifically been mentioned in any of the cases, the Copyright Act has been held to provide protection similar to that right, particularly as construed by the Supreme Court with respect to unpublished material. And although the Court acknowledged the possibility that an unauthorized user could prove fair use of an unpublished work, it indicated that such circumstances would be rare since "publication of an author's expression before he has authorized its dissemination seriously infringes the author's right to decide when and whether it will be made public." (As discussed above, the "fair use" aspect of that observation was altered by Congress in 1992.)

The federal trademark law, the Lanham Act, has been the source of successful arguments for protection akin to the right of paternity and particularly that law's prohibition against the dissemination of works that contain a "false designation of origin." The Lanham Act permits claims on behalf of creators where false authorship credit is being given, even if trademark rights and market competition are not directly involved. In one case, the court held for a plaintiff who complained that credit was falsely given to the defendant as preparer and editor of a book. However, most of the effort to secure *droit moral* protection in the United States has involved rights akin to the right of integrity.

Every state has laws against "unfair competition," and to some extent such laws may be invoked to prevent the "misappropriation" of a creator's work. In two cases involving motion pictures, a right similar to the *droit moral* right of integrity was found to protect filmmakers whose films were severely edited for television. The question was whether the artist had contracted away "mutilation" rights. Other state laws that might come into play are those involving defamation—for example, where the attribution of a distorted version of a work to an artist damages her reputation. And the Lanham Act has also been useful with respect to the right of integrity.

In one important case, the Monty Python group sought an injunction against a television network that intended to broadcast severely edited versions of three of its programs, even though the network had obtained permission from the group to air the programs. The group contended that the network's editing "impaired the integrity" of its work and that this violated the permission the network had obtained and the legal rights of the group.

The federal court of appeals in New York ruled that "the unauthorized editing of the underlying work, if proven, would constitute an infringement of the copyright in that work similar to any other use of a work that exceeded the license granted by the proprietor of the copyright." Even more significantly, the court declared that it seemed likely the group would establish that "the cuts made constituted an actionable mutilation of Monty Python's work." This legal claim, the court said, "finds its roots in the continental concept of *droit moral*, or moral right, which may generally be summarized as including the right of the artist to have his work attributed to him in the form in which he created it." The court continued:

> American copyright law, as presently written, does not recognize moral rights or provide a cause of action for their violation, since the law seeks to vindicate the economic, rather than the personal rights of authors. Nevertheless, the economic incentive for artistic and intellectual creation that serves as the foundation for American copyright law . . . cannot be reconciled with the inability of artists to obtain relief for mutilation or misrepresentation of their work to the public on which the artists are financially dependent. Thus courts have long granted relief for misrepresentation of an artist's work by relying on theories outside the statutory law of copyright, such as contract law or the tort of unfair competition. Although such decisions are clothed in terms of proprietary right in one's creation, they also properly vindicate the author's personal right to prevent the presentation of his work to the public in a distorted form.

The court indicated that the "garbled" editing of the group's work violated its rights under the Lanham Act, which protects against "misrepresentations that may injure [a person's] business or personal reputation, even where no registered trademark is concerned." The court concluded, "It is sufficient to violate the [Lanham] Act that a representation of a product, although technically true, creates a false impression of the product's origin." Although the language the court used strongly suggests that authors and artists have significant legal protection for the integrity of their work apart from copyright, and although such protection is to be desired, this case is somewhat unusual, and alas such protection is generally not available in this country today. The broad declarations of the Monty Python case have not been applied to enough situations where creators have suffered similar injury to lead to many useful legal precedents. For these rights to be truly meaningful, legislative action is necessary.

Have any *droit moral* laws been passed in the United States?

In 1979 California was the first state to enact an "Art Preservation Act," protecting works of "fine art" (defined to include "an original painting, sculpture, or drawing, or an original work of art in glass, of recognized quality" but not a work "prepared under contract for commercial use by its purchaser"). That law stated that "the Legislature hereby finds and declares that the physical alteration or destruction of fine art, which is an expression of the artist's personality, is detrimental to the artist's reputation, and artists therefore have an interest in protecting their works of fine art against any alteration or destruction; and that there is also a public interest in preserving the integrity of cultural and artistic creations." Other states, including New York, also enacted similar laws, and in 1990 the U.S. Congress enacted the "Visual Artists Rights Act" (VARA), which was subsequently found to preempt most if not all of those state laws.

In the United States, moral rights receive their strongest protection under VARA. VARA applies to "works of visual art," which are defined as paintings, drawings, prints, sculptures, and photographs, existing in a single copy or a limited edition of 200 signed and numbered copies or fewer." To be protected, a photograph must have been taken for exhibition purposes only. Posters, maps, globes, motion pictures, electronic publications, and applied art are among the categories of visual works denied protection. Also excluded are works made for hire. VARA provides:

> [T]he author of a work of visual art (1) shall have the right (A) to claim authorship of that work, and (B) to prevent the use of his or her name as the author of any work of visual art which he or she did not create; (2) shall have the right to prevent the use of his or her name as the author of the work of visual art in the event of a distortion, mutilation, or other modification of the work which would be prejudicial to his or her honor or reputation; and (3) subject to [specified] limitations shall have the right (A) to prevent any intentional distortion, mutilation, or other modification of that work which would be prejudicial to his or her honor or reputation, and any intentional distortion, mutilation, or modification of that work is a violation of that right, and (B) to prevent any destruction of a work of recognized stature, and any intentional or grossly negligent destruction of that work is a violation of that right.

Further, VARA provides that "Only the author of a work of visual art has the rights conferred by subsection (a) in that work, whether or not the author is the copyright owner" and that "The authors of a joint work of visual art are co-owners of the rights conferred by subsection (a) in that work."

The courts have interpreted VARA narrowly. For example, in one case involving 27 sculptures in a park the court concluded that whether VARA protects a work of art is to be construed "narrowly" and that because many of the elements of the park were not created specifically by the sculptor, his works didn't qualify. VARA also specifies that it only applies during the life of the creator, and not, as in the case of most other rights under the Copyright Act, for a period of years after the creator's death. Therefore, if one mutilates a work of art by a living artist, VARA applies, but if one mutilates a work by a deceased artist, VARA will not apply.

In VARA cases involving the destruction of a work of visual art, the key issue is what constitutes a "work of recognized stature," which is required for protection. Unfortunately, there is no clear definition of that term and the courts decide on a case-by-case basis whether to consider proffered evidence of "stature." Most courts require expert testimony from members of the art community, but others will rely on letters and newspaper articles. New and emerging artists are likely to have the most difficulty proving the required "stature."

In one famous case, the owners of an unused factory allowed artists to spray paint its outer walls. When the owners decided to raze the building, several artists sought an injunction to prevent the demolition. The court framed the question as whether "the work of an exterior aerosol artist—given its general ephemeral nature—is worthy of any protection under the law." But the court interestingly made findings about the relative quality of the graffiti over time, characterizing it as "distasteful" at the start but later of "vastly improved" quality when a "curator" undertook to regulate it. Ultimately, the court concluded that while the factory constitutes visual art, it is not a "work of visual art" within VARA.

Finally, VARA provides that its protections "may not be transferred" but "may be waived if the author expressly agrees to such a waiver in a written instrument signed by the author" and that any transfer of the underlying work "shall not constitute a waiver of [those] rights."

For works of art not protected by VARA, trademark (and related) laws may provide some protection. For example, if someone presents another's work as her own, or conversely presents her own work as that of another, the laws against "unfair competition" may apply. Also, if a creator's work is so well known as to be recognized as being by that creator, a distortion or alteration of the work may constitute trademark "dilution." But like copyright law, trademark law also contains a "fair use" exception, which in particular cases may trump the otherwise available legal protection.

Although decidedly limited in its scope, VARA represents the first recognition of *droit moral* rights on the federal level and may yet inspire the development of more such rights, on the federal and state levels.

Beyond VARA and trademark law, there are other possible mechanisms that a creator may be able to use to enforce at least some moral rights. For example, a creator may show that, by altering or distorting her work, a "derivative work" was created, which would violate the creator's rights under the Copyright Act. Also, if a work is falsely attributed to a creator, she may have an action for defamation. Or if a person adopts the identity of a creator, or that creator's work, there may be a claim for violation of the creator's "right of publicity," for "misappropriation," or for "unjust enrichment."

What about the controversy surrounding the "colorizing" of old movies? Did that involve *droit moral*?

Yes, although not directly in this country. Since the people doing the colorizing had acquired the necessary copyright rights to the films (or the films were in the public domain), no copyright issues were directly involved. Those opposing the practice—including the directors and writers of the films being colorized without their consent or approval—claimed the practice violated their artistic integrity. But while their objections were deeply felt and urgently expressed, no court challenge to the practice has been successful in this country. However, John Huston's heirs did bring suit in France, objecting to a plan to distribute there a colorized version of *The Asphalt Jungle*, which was directed by Huston. In 1991, France's highest court ruled that the creators' *droit moral* supported an injunction against the showing of the colorized movie.

Are there any other ways trademark and unfair competition laws can be useful to creators?

Short phrases and titles, which are not eligible for federal copyright protection, may be protected by federal trademark law and the trademark and unfair competition laws of the states. A phrase like "Heeeere's Johnny!" or a title like *Gone with the Wind* will almost certainly be entitled to protection by such (non-copyright) laws, which have as their purpose preventing customer confusion or the erosion of the value of a name or identity. The principal requirement for such protection is that the phrase or title be "distinctive" and be associated in the public's mind with a particular source or a particular work. This means that the title of a literary work will not be entitled to protection unless and until it has achieved such a direct association, which the law calls "secondary meaning."

Can a creator protect ideas, as such, before they are published?

Yes, to some extent. Copyright does not protect ideas, and once they are publicly disclosed, they are in the public domain. But this does not mean that those ideas have no value before they are disclosed or that an author is powerless to protect them from unauthorized use. It is obvious that ideas can have enormous value. Countless books, movies, TV shows, and advertising campaigns owe much of their success to an underlying idea. Under certain circumstances, the law will protect the creators of such ideas from misappropriation, wholly apart from copyright. For example, if a creator discloses an idea under circumstances where it is understood (or should have been understood) that it would be kept confidential or that the creator would be compensated if it was used following disclosure, the law may treat those "understandings" as "contracts" and permit the creator to recover for their breach.

In some cases, these contracts will be "implied" by the conduct of the parties; in others, they will be "implied" by the law as construed by the courts. It may also be possible in appropriate cases to recover for unauthorized use where there has been no disclosure—for example, where the idea has truly been stolen—but there are few precedents to support such relief and the burden of proof on the plaintiff would be very high, since the courts recognize that the same or similar ideas can often be devised independently and that many people erroneously assume that an idea similar to theirs "must have been stolen."

What can a creator do to protect ideas before they are disclosed?

First, the creator should put the idea in writing as fully as possible. This will ensure that at least the creator's expression of the idea will be protected by copyright and may also discourage others from trying to distinguish between the copyrightable expression and the non-copyrightable idea. Second, the creator should date the writing and take steps to establish proof of that date—by mailing a copy to herself or another person and keeping the envelope sealed; by having the date notarized or otherwise confirmed by a trusted other person, such as an agent or lawyer; or by filing the writing with a group like the Authors Guild (if the creator is a member) that will be able to confirm the date of filing. This establishes when the creator had the idea, which may be crucial if the dispute involves who had the idea first. Third, the creator should be extremely careful to whom and under what circumstances the idea is disclosed. The idea should be disclosed only when it is understood that the creator is not gratuitously relinquishing it but expects to be compensated if it is used. If the creator signs a release waiving any such expectation (and such releases are frequently demanded) or makes the disclosure knowing that the recipient has no obligation to pay if the idea is used, the creator may be without legal recourse if the idea is used following that disclosure. Conversely, whenever possible the creator should have the receiving party sign a "nondisclosure agreement" (NDA) promising not to disclose any idea disclosed by the creator.

CHAPTER 3

LIBEL, PRIVACY, OBSCENITY, AND OTHER POSSIBLE LEGAL RISKS

Most nonfiction writers, and many fiction writers as well, are directly affected by the law of libel and privacy, among other legal risks. Even photographers and other visual artists can be confronted by claims in these areas. In addition, especially in recent years, creative people have been accused of causing injury to plaintiffs in other ways by the publication of their works. It is important that authors, artists, and other creative people understand the nature and extent of these claims and how to deal with them.

LIBEL RISKS

What is the purpose of the law of libel?

As the Supreme Court has put it, "The legitimate state interest underlying the law of libel is the compensation of individuals for the harm inflicted on them by defamatory falsehoods. The individual's right to the protection of his good name 'reflects no more than our basic concept of the essential dignity and worth of every human being—a concept at the root of any decent system of ordered liberty.'"

Nevertheless, it has been argued, by no less than late Supreme Court Justices Hugo Black and William O. Douglas, among others, that any law of libel violates the freedoms of speech and press guaranteed by the First Amendment. This view has not been accepted by any American court or legislature and is not likely to be in the foreseeable future.

But this is not to say that the First Amendment is irrelevant to the law of libel. In 1964 the U.S. Supreme Court ruled for the first time that libel cases directly implicate the essential freedoms of speech and the press that are protected by the First Amendment; since then, the Court has substantially rewritten much of libel law to reconcile it with those precious First Amendment freedoms. The major changes imposed by the Supreme Court on the law of libel will be discussed later in this chapter.

When can a statement give rise to a successful libel claim?

The answer varies with the nature of the statement, the speaker, the subject, the claimed injury, and other factors, including the particular law that will apply. In short, there is no short answer.

However, it is possible to list six requirements that must almost always be established before a statement can result in a successful libel suit: (1) The statement must be libelous (or defamatory); (2) It must be false; (3) It must be about ("of and concerning") the living person claiming to be libeled; (4) It must be "published"; (5) It must be published with "fault"; and (6) It must cause actual injury to the plaintiff.

What is meant by libel?

Libel and slander together compose what the law calls "defamation." Libelous statements are in writing or otherwise set down in concrete non-ephemeral form; slanderous statements are generally oral and lack concreteness. It is unlikely that creators will be confronted by claims of slander, so this chapter will be primarily concerned with libel.

A libelous statement must tend "to harm the reputation of another as to lower him in the estimation of the community or to deter third persons from associating or dealing with him." Expanded and formalized somewhat, "it must be an accusation against the character of a person . . . which affects his reputation, in that it tends to hold him up to ridicule, contempt, shame, disgrace or obloquy, to degrade him in the estimation of the community, to induce an evil opinion of him in the minds of right thinking persons, to make him an object of reproach, to diminish his respectability or abridge his comforts, to change his position in society for the worse, to dishonor or discredit him in the estimation of the public, or his friends and acquaintances, or to deprive him of friendly intercourse in society, or cause him to be shunned or avoided."

In short, a libelous statement is one that tends to injure a person's reputation. However, a great many statements that appear to provide the basis for a libel suit (as lawyers say, to be "actionable") are protected by the law.

What kinds of statements may be found libelous?

The libelousness of a statement depends on its relation to the reputation of its subject. As further discussed on the next page, it is conceivable that any statement about another, even one that appears to be laudatory, can be libelous.

The law has historically recognized four major categories of potentially libelous statements, and although those categories are not conclusive or all-encompassing, they are useful examples of the imputations that are most often alleged to be libelous: assertions of (1) crime, (2) loathsome diseases, (3) incompetence or dishonesty in one's business or profession and (4) unchastity in a woman. On the face of it, the false charge that a woman is "an AIDS-laden prostitute who regularly cheats her clients" could give rise to a claim of libel. However, as we shall see, even this statement might not result in a libel judgment.

If the libelous nature of a statement is apparent from the statement itself, it is considered libelous "per se," and the law does not require further proof of the defamatory nature of the statement. (Fault, injury, and damages, among other issues, would still have to be established; those issues are discussed more fully later in this chapter.)

Can a statement that seems innocent be libelous?

Sometimes, if it is false, even a seemingly innocent statement can injure its subject's reputation. For example, the false statement that a woman was the guest of honor at a lavish dinner at a Steak and Brew restaurant could be found libelous if it turned out that she is the president of the local branch of Vegetarian Teetotalers. Similarly, the false statement that John Smith is a "distinguished war hero" could be found libelous if Mr. Smith is an avowed lifelong pacifist.

When, as with these examples, the libelous nature of the statement must be established by extrinsic facts, this is referred to as libel "per quod." It is obviously much more difficult to guard against this category of libel than against libel per se. For this reason, among others, the law in most states requires a plaintiff claiming to have been libeled by extrinsic facts to prove that he has sustained specific (special) damages as a result of the statement, not merely injury to his general reputation. The issue of special damages is discussed more fully later in this chapter.

Can a true statement be libelous?

Probably not, although the law in some states may suggest the contrary. Under libel law as it existed before the Supreme Court revolutionized large parts of it, defamatory statements were "presumed" false. The burden was on the libel defendant to prove that they were true, which was not always easy.

In the years since 1964, however, the law has become clear (at least where the alleged libel arose out of publication through the "media") that the person claiming libel (the plaintiff) must prove that the statement is false. Moreover, it has long been the law that substantially true statements cannot give rise to successful claims of libel. The plaintiff must prove not merely that the statement is not completely true in every particular but that it is substantially false in its material elements.

Can a person be libeled by implication?

Yes, at least under certain circumstances. And although the law in different states may vary in important ways, an important recent decision by a federal trial court in New York provided this useful summary:

[W]here a plaintiff asserts a defamation claim based not on any alleged falsity of the statements themselves, but on an alleged defamatory implication that could be derived from the unchallenged facts, the Court will require an "especially rigorous showing" that (1) the language may be reasonably read to impart the false innuendo, and (2) the author intends or endorses the inference . . . The alleged innuendo "may not enlarge upon the meaning of words so as to convey a meaning that is not expressed." . . . To the extent that [the plaintiff] alleges that the implication arises due to the omission of certain facts, the Court will look to whether such omission would materially change the alleged implication or render untrue what is otherwise unchallenged.

Under this statement of the law, the statement that "John Smith was recently seen purchasing a crowbar and in the following days there were several forcible home break-ins in his neighborhood" could be entirely true but still be actionable—but only if Smith can show that the speaker "intended" or "endorsed" the implication that he was responsible for the break-ins. And in most—less blatant—claims of libel-by-implication, that will usually be difficult to prove.

Can a statement of opinion be libelous?

Yes and no. Although the Supreme Court has reiterated in several cases that only a false statement of "fact" can give rise to a successful libel claim, it also made it clear that statements of "opinion" under certain circumstances can result in legal liability.

The Supreme Court once grandly stated that "Under the First Amendment there is no such thing as a false idea. However pernicious an opinion may seem, we depend for its correction not on the conscience of judges and juries but on the competition of other ideas." But it is now clear that the law on this issue is much more nuanced.

The same federal court that provided the summary of "libel-by-implication" quoted above also provided this very clear and useful summary of the law governing claims of libelous opinions:

> As many courts have observed, the "seemingly simple" proposition that expressions of opinion are protected "belies an often complicated task of distinguishing between potentially actionable statements of fact and nonactionable expressions of opinion." . . . New York courts look principally to three factors to make this determination: (1) whether the specific language in issue has a precise meaning which is readily understood; (2) whether the statements are capable of being proven true or false; and (3) whether either the . . . full context of the communication in which the statement appears or the broader social context and surrounding circumstances are such as to signal readers or listeners that what is being read or heard is likely to be opinion, not fact. . . .
>
> Often, statements of "rhetorical hyperbole" or "imaginative expression" are held not actionable, because they "cannot reasonably be interpreted as stating actual facts" that could be proved false. . . . A statement of "pure opinion" is one which is either

"accompanied by a recitation of the facts upon which it is based" or "does not imply that it is based upon undisclosed facts." . . . However, if a statement "impl[ies] that the speaker's opinion is based on the speaker's knowledge of facts that are not disclosed to the reader," then it may be actionable. . . . Such statements may be actionable "not because they convey 'false opinions' but rather because a reasonable listener or reader would infer that the speaker or writer knows certain facts, unknown to the audience, which support the opinion and are detrimental to the person toward whom the communication is directed.". . .

In other words, a statement of opinion that is based on undisclosed facts is potentially actionable because it carries with it an implicit statement of those facts. On the other hand, "a proffered hypothesis that is offered after a full recitation of the facts on which it is based is readily understood by the audience as conjecture."

With that statement of the law as our guide, it becomes clear that the following statements could—or could not—be actionable libels: "Jim Adams is a corrupt liar and thief"; "Sally Smith has Nazi sympathies"; and "Tom Brady knew about those deflated balls." The outcome of hypothetical libel cases based on those statements will depend on a close application of the legal rules quoted above.

What about epithets and hyperbole?

It's probably fair to say that the more exaggerated and extreme, the less likely such statements will be found actionable. In one leading case involving a reference to the plaintiff as one of "those bastards," a federal court of appeals rejected the claim libel, declaring:

> It is perfectly apparent that these words were used as mere epithets, as terms of abuse and opprobrium. As such they had no real meaning except to indicate that the individual who used them was under a strong emotional feeling of dislike toward those about whom he used them. Not being intended or understood as statements of fact they are impossible of proof or disproof. Indeed, such words of vituperation and abuse reflect more on the character of the user than they do on that of the individual to whom they are intended to refer. It has long been settled that such words are not of themselves actionable as libelous.

In another case, the plaintiff's bargaining position in a dispute with the local government was characterized as "blackmail." The Supreme Court rejected the claim of libel, stating:

> It is simply impossible to believe that a reader who reached the word "blackmail" in either article would not have understood exactly what was meant: it was [plaintiff's] public and wholly legal negotiating proposals that were being criticized. No reader could have thought that either the speakers at the meetings or the newspaper articles reporting their words were charging [plaintiff] with the commission of a criminal offense. On the contrary, even the most careless reader must have perceived that the word was no more than rhetorical hyperbole, a vigorous epithet

used by those who considered [plaintiff's] negotiating position extremely unreasonable. Indeed, the record is completely devoid of evidence that anyone in the city . . . or anywhere else thought [plaintiff] had been charged with a crime.

Similarly, in 1988 the Supreme Court unanimously found that an ad parody in *Hustler* magazine that portrayed the Reverend Jerry Falwell as having had sex with his mother in an outhouse "could not reasonably have been interpreted as stating actual facts about the public figure involved."

But not every epithet is immune from a claim of libel. In a 2016 case involving scientists on opposite sides of the climate change debate, an appeals court found the assertion that the plaintiff was the "poster boy of the corrupt and disgraced climate science echo chamber" and that he engaged in "wrongdoing," "deceptions," "data manipulation," and "academic and scientific misconduct and called him the Jerry Sandusky of climate science," comparing the plaintiff's "molest[ing] and tortur[ing] data in the service of politicized science" to Sandusky's "molesting children" were all actionable as libel. The court explained:

A jury could find that the article accuses Dr. Mann of engaging in specific acts of academic and scientific misconduct in the manipulation of data, and thus conveys a defamatory meaning, because "to constitute a libel it is enough that the defamatory utterance imputes any misconduct whatever in the conduct of [plaintiff's] calling." Moreover, a jury could find that by calling Dr. Mann "the [Jerry] Sandusky of climate science," the article implied that Dr. Mann's manipulation of data was seriously deviant for a scientist. These noxious comparisons, a jury could find, would demean Dr. Mann's scientific reputation and lower his standing in the community by making him appear similarly "odious, infamous, or ridiculous."

Who can sue for libel?

Only people who are alive at the time of publication can sue for libel. The law considers that the interest in one's reputation that the law of libel is designed to protect no longer applies when a person dies; as a result, it is generally impossible to libel the dead. Corporations, partnerships, associations, and the like also have protectable interests in their reputations, but usually to a more limited extent than those of living people. Such entities can sue for libels that affect their financial credit or standing in their fields or that cast aspersions on their honesty or on the quality or integrity of their products.

Must a person be named to sue for libel?

No, but the plaintiff must prove that the alleged libel refers to her—in the language of the law, that the words are "of and concerning" her. Obviously, a named person meets this requirement. Several persons may have the same name as the person named in an alleged libel, and it has happened that a person other than the one intended has successfully sued.

Without being named, a person can sometimes prove that the libel is "of and concerning" him. For example, a libelous reference to "the only dentist in town" will be found to apply to the person who meets that description; a reference to "a Main Street dentist" will be found to apply to the dentist who can prove that he is the only dentist on Main Street.

Can members of groups sue for libelous statements about their groups?

Generally, no. The courts have consistently held that a libelous statement about a large group (e.g., "All Lithuanians are child molesters" or "All Republicans cheat on their taxes") does not refer to each member of that group.

Nevertheless, it may be possible for a group member to sue successfully for libel. If the context of the statement indicates that the plaintiff was its intended target (e.g., if the statement "All lawyers are thieves" is made in an article about one lawyer), the plaintiff may be found to have been libeled by the general statement. Similarly, the courts have been willing to find group members libeled if the group is small enough to justify the conclusion that the members were effectively referred to. As a leading authority has concluded, "While it is not possible to set definite limits as to the size of the group or class . . . the cases in which recovery has been allowed usually have involved numbers of 25 or fewer."

Must a statement be published to give rise to a successful libel claim?

Yes. The most libelous statement imaginable cannot give rise to a successful libel claim if it remains in the author's manuscript (or diary) and is not published to anybody else. The traditional rule is that a statement is published if it is shown to a person other than the subject of the libel. A letter from A to B in which B is seriously libeled does not enable B to sue A for libel, unless, for example, A dictated the letter to her secretary.

What about someone (not the originator) who repeats or reports a libelous statement?

The traditional rule is that anyone who repeats, republishes, or distributes a libelous statement made by another can be held legally responsible, which technically means that the printer and seller of an allegedly libelous work can be sued. But this rule has been significantly modified in recent years.

First, the law now requires that a plaintiff prove that a libelous statement was published with some degree of "fault," which means at least that it was published negligently. It is conceivable, and in some cases probable, that the repeater of a libelous statement will be found to have acted reasonably, even if the original speaker has not, and thus cannot be held liable. This would almost always be the case with respect to printers, sellers, and others who did not participate in the origination of the libel.

Second, a few courts have extended a special protection from liability to those who repeat libelous statements in the course of reporting on newsworthy subjects, even if the writer knows the statement is false or has serious doubts about its truth. Most conspicuously, this legal protection has been established for the accurate (or "fair") repetition—for example in press accounts—of libelous statements made during official governmental proceedings such as trials, legislative hearings, or debates. This "qualified privilege" is discussed more fully below.

When is a libelous statement insulated from legal liability?

Whenever the law (the courts and the legislative branches of government) decides that the public interest requires that certain otherwise libelous statements be protected. Then the libelous statements are "cloaked with a privilege."

How many kinds of privilege does the law provide?

Two. An "absolute privilege" completely protects a libelous statement from legal action, regardless of circumstances, motive, or injury caused. A "qualified privilege" cloaks a libelous statement with a legal immunity that can be overcome by showing that the maker of the statement "abused" the privilege. The burden is generally on the plaintiff to prove this.

What kinds of statements are protected by an absolute privilege?

Statements made in the course of official governmental activities may be so protected. This includes statements made in judicial proceedings, including those by judges, attorneys, parties, witnesses, and jurors. In general, statements by federal and state legislators are also protected if made in connection with their official duties, although this is not as clear for lesser legislative bodies. In the executive branch, statements made by high federal and state officials are generally protected. But this is less clear for lower-level officials and units of government.

Outside the government, otherwise libelous statements made by one spouse to the other are generally protected by an absolute privilege, as are statements that are made with the consent of their subjects.

It is important to remember, however, that absolute privilege only applies to a statement made in a privileged setting and is generally not available if the statement is repeated outside the setting, whether the repetition is by the original speaker or someone else. Such repetitions may, however, be protected by a qualified (conditional) privilege.

When are statements protected by a qualified privilege?

Basically, when it is considered more important to encourage (and protect) the making of statements that may be false and libelous than to allow victims of such statements to recover damages for libel. A qualified privilege generally applies only if the statement is made in good faith, consistent with the purposes that gave rise to the privilege. Examples include statements to proper authorities accusing another person of a crime or other improper conduct (unethical conduct by a doctor or lawyer, physical abuse by a policeman) and statements made by credit reporting agencies and private detectives to clients.

Of special interest to writers is the qualified privilege that protects "fair" reports of governmental statements (which themselves are protected by an absolute privilege). As one legal authority has summarized it, "The publication of defamatory matter concerning another in a report of an official action or proceeding or of a meeting open to the public that deals with a matter of public concern is privileged if the report is accurate and complete or a fair abridgement of the occurrence reported." A fair report in a book or newspaper article that Tom Brown testified during the trial of his lawsuit against his partner Bill Jackson that Jackson embezzled money from the firm, cheated clients, and was always drunk is privileged even if the testimony is false and Brown and the writer knew or suspected it was false. But if the report is not "fair"—if the charges are taken out of context, are erroneously reported, or are reported to be true—then the author and publisher can be successfully sued for libel.

A 2017 decision by a New York trial court demonstrates the "liberality" of the "fair report" privilege. A libel suit was brought based in part on a headline that read: DRUNK DRIVING-POTHEAD THINKS HE'S FIT TO BE A CORRECTIONS OFFICER. The Court stated in part:

[The] headline is unfortunate, sensationalist and drafted simply to garner attention. But the headline and the article, when considered together as one document, can only be characterized as a fair and true report of the substantive issues in plaintiff's [lawsuit challenging his rejection for employment]. The article makes clear that the marijuana charges were dropped and documents plaintiff's insistence he did not drive while drunk. This conclusion is further supported when viewing the article with the requisite degree of liberality . . . When considering the article in its entirety, the presence of an inaccurate statement does not require a finding that [the "fair report" statute] does not apply.

How has the Supreme Court changed the law of libel?

Dramatically. Before 1964, a libelous statement was presumed to be false. The plaintiff was virtually assured of victory once he established that a libelous statement had been published about him unless the maker of the statement could prove that the statement was true, protected by a privilege, or caused the plaintiff no injury.

Against that background, one L.B. Sullivan, an elected commissioner of Montgomery, Alabama, sued the *New York Times* and four black Alabama clergymen because of what he considered libelous references to him (even though he wasn't named) in a full-page advertisement signed by a number of civil rights leaders (including the four Alabama defendants) that sought support for the civil rights movement in the South. Applying the traditional law of libel, a Montgomery jury awarded Sullivan $500,000 in damages (the full amount requested), and the award was upheld by the Alabama appellate courts.

A unanimous Supreme Court found that the traditional libel rules that gave rise to that result violate the protections for speech and press in the First Amendment. The Court set aside the jury's award and declared that to recover for libel, a public official like Sullivan would have to satisfy much more stringent legal requirements.

In reaching that conclusion the Court, speaking through Justice William J. Brennan Jr., observed that "freedom of expression upon public questions is secured by the First Amendment" and that this constitutional safeguard "was fashioned to assure unfettered interchange of ideas for the bringing about of political and social changes desired by the people." As a result, Brennan wrote, "we consider this case against the background of a profound national commitment to the principle that debate on public issues should be uninhibited, robust, and wide-open, and that it may well include vehement, caustic, and sometimes unpleasantly sharp attacks on government and public officials." He continued: "The present advertisement, as an expression of grievance and protest on one of the major public issues of our time, would seem clearly to qualify for the constitutional protection. The question is whether it forfeits that protection by the falsity of some of its factual statements and by its alleged defamation of respondent."

The Court stated that some factual error is "inevitable in free debate" and that such error "must be protected if the freedoms of expression are to have the 'breathing space' that they 'need . . . to survive.'" It added that the defamatory nature of such criticism of public officials does not alter this: "Criticism of official conduct does not lose its constitutional protection merely because it is effective criticism and hence diminishes their official reputations." It was not enough that the Alabama libel law allowed the defense of truth:

A rule compelling the critic of official conduct to guarantee the truth of all his factual assertions—and to do so on pain of libel judgments virtually unlimited in amount—leads to . . . "self-censorship." Allowance of the defense of truth, with the burden of proving it on the defendant, does not mean that only false speech will be deterred. . . . Under such a rule, would-be critics of official conduct may be deterred from voicing their criticism, even though it is believed to be true and even though it is in fact true, because of doubt whether it can be proved in court or fear of the expense of having to do so. . . . The rule thus dampens the vigor and limits the variety of public debate. It is inconsistent with the First and Fourteenth Amendments.

In what may be the most important sentence in the law of libel, the Court rewrote a significant part of that law: "The constitutional guarantees require, we think, a federal rule that prohibits a public official from recovering damages for a defamatory falsehood relating to his official conduct unless he proves that the statement was made with 'actual malice'—that is, with knowledge that it was false or with reckless disregard of whether it was false or not." From then on, at least as far as public official libel plaintiffs were concerned, the rules of the game were different indeed.

What does "actual malice" mean?

The term "actual malice" as used by the Supreme Court is confusing and does not mean what most people think it means. As one federal judge put it, "'Actual malice' is . . . a term of art having nothing to do with actual malice."

In the *New York Times* case, the Court indicated that actual malice means that a statement alleged to be libelous was made "with knowledge that it was false or with reckless disregard of whether it was false or not." Later, the Court elaborated, indicating that actual malice required a "high degree of awareness of [the statement's] probable falsity"; "either deliberate falsification or reckless publication despite the publisher's awareness of probable falsity"; "sufficient evidence to permit the conclusion that the defendant in fact entertained serious doubts as to the truth of his publication"; and "subjective awareness of probable falsity."

It is clear that negligence (which simply means acting in an "unreasonable" or careless way) is not actual malice. Misremembering the facts underlying an event, failing to confirm the substance of a story, or relying on a source that turns out to be unreliable, which may constitute negligence, does not qualify as actual malice in the absence of proof that the author "entertained serious doubts as to the truth of his publication." In an important decision in which the federal court of appeals in California overturned a $5 million judgment in favor of entertainer Wayne Newton against NBC, the court stated: "Even an extreme departure from accepted professional standards of journalism will not suffice to establish actual malice; nor will any other departure from reasonably prudent conduct, including the failure to investigate before publishing." Further, proof of malice in its commonsense (and common-law) meaning—"hatred, ill will or enmity or a wanton desire to injure"—does not in itself prove actual malice.

How has "reckless disregard" been defined?

Besides "knowledge of falsity," the *New York Times* standard provides for recovery in case of "reckless disregard of the truth or falsity" of a defamatory statement. Obviously, reckless disregard is a looser concept than actual knowledge of falsity. It means that the publisher entertained serious doubts and then without further checking or adequate verification published the material while continuing to harbor those doubts.

Under the Supreme Court's decisions, a finding of "recklessness" depends on the publisher's subjective state of mind and not an objective determination of whether a reasonably prudent person would have published the material. However, mere "professions of good faith" will not necessarily defeat liability "when the publisher's allegations are so inherently improbable that only a reckless man would have put them in circulation."

Likewise, recklessness may be found where there are obvious reasons to doubt the veracity of the informant or the accuracy of his reports. In a major case, the Supreme Court reaffirmed the subjective nature of the "recklessness" requirement, stating: "Although the concept of 'reckless disregard' cannot be fully encompassed in one infallible definition, . . . we have made clear that the defendant must have made the false publication with a 'high degree of awareness of . . . probable falsity,' . . . or must have 'entertained serious doubts as to the truth of his publication.'" In the same case, the Court also said, "Although courts must be careful not to place too much reliance on such factors, a plaintiff is entitled to prove the defendant's state of mind through circumstantial evidence, . . . and it cannot be said that evidence concerning motive or care never bears any relation to the actual malice inquiry."

How has actual malice been established in libel actions?

It is difficult to establish that an author or publisher published a statement whose truth she seriously doubted. The threshold of proof is high to protect freedom of expression.

Still, libel plaintiffs have been able to establish actual malice; for example, a widely publicized action brought by the celebrity Carol Burnett against the *National Enquirer* resulted in a $1.6-million jury verdict against the *Enquirer*, which was subsequently reduced to $200,000. The falsity of the article, which strongly implied that Ms. Burnett was drunk, rowdy, and caused a disturbance with Henry Kissinger in a Washington, DC, restaurant, was not in dispute. And there was, according to the trial and appeals courts, sufficient proof that the *Enquirer*'s gossip columnist had serious doubts about the truth of the publication. Indeed, according to the trial court, "There is a high degree of probability that [the editor] fabricated part of the publication [relating to Henry Kissinger]." Moreover, in attempting to verify the story received from a "freelance tipster," there was uncontradicted evidence that the editor was warned of the tipster's unreliability and that witnesses at the scene gave the editor information that substantially contradicted the tipster's story. The story was nonetheless published without removing the defamatory information.

In another case, the Supreme Court affirmed a finding that a newspaper acted with actual malice in an article about a candidate in a local election. Among the factors emphasized by the Court were the paper's failure to listen to tape recordings supplied by the candidate that he said would support his position and the paper's failure to make any attempt to interview a key witness in the underlying dispute. As the Court put it: "Although failure to investigate will not alone support a finding of actual malice, . . . the purposeful avoidance of the truth is in a different category."

In a much-discussed case, the Supreme Court held that a writer's alteration of statements directly attributed in quotation marks to the plaintiff can constitute actual malice, at least under certain circumstances. The case involved a profile of Jeffrey

Masson, an outspoken critic of the institutions of psychoanalysis, written by Janet Malcolm and published first in the *New Yorker* magazine and then in a book published by Alfred A. Knopf, Inc. In a suit for libel, Masson claimed that Malcolm had fabricated numerous statements that were set forth as spoken by him and that as attributed to him the statements were libelous. The defendants denied that any quotations were fabricated, and that issue had not been resolved. The lower courts held that actual malice could not be found even if the quotations were fabricated since they were "rational interpretations" of things Masson might have said.

The issue before the Supreme Court was the extent to which the deliberate alteration or fabrication of quotes attributed to the plaintiff can constitute actual malice. To the relief of many in the publishing community, the Court acknowledged that quotations are frequently altered in the publishing process and that the fact of alteration alone could not establish actual malice. Instead, the Court held that "a deliberate alteration of the words uttered by a plaintiff does not equate with knowledge of falsity . . . unless the alteration results in a material change in the meaning conveyed by the statement." The Court returned Masson's suit to the lower courts for a determination whether that new test had been met and whether the magazine and book publishers of the profile could be found liable under it.

In what situations has actual malice not been established?

Plaintiffs have failed in many cases to meet this demanding standard. Among allegations that have failed to prove actual malice are these: publication of "emotionally tinged" documents; insufficient checking or verification of the details of a news story; negligence combined with hostility toward the plaintiff; mere ill will toward the plaintiff; and political or editorial bias.

Who qualifies as a "public official"?

In the *Times* case, an elected city commissioner was held to be a public official. Subsequently, the courts have found a mayor, a former public recreation area supervisor, a county attorney, an elected clerk of a county court, a police chief, a deputy sheriff, and a candidate for public office to be public officials. However, the Supreme Court has emphasized that while it has "not provided precise boundaries for the category of 'public official,' it cannot be thought to include all public employees." In the important *Gertz* case (discussed on the following pages), the Court had no difficulty finding that being a lawyer (hence an "officer of the court") and membership on committees appointed by a big-city mayor do not make a libel plaintiff a public official. A California case held that a public school teacher was not a public official. However, other cases have found teachers to be public officials.

For whatever guidance this provides, the Supreme Court has said, "The 'public official' designation applies at the very least to those among the hierarchy of government employees who have, or appear to the public to have, substantial responsibility for or control over the conduct of government affairs."

The Court has ruled that the protection of allegedly libelous statements about public officials applies to statements made after the official has left office. But the Court added, without further elaboration, that there may be cases where the plaintiff is so far removed from a former position of authority that comment on the way in which he performed his responsibilities no longer has the interest necessary to justify the *Times* rule.

Are all statements about public officials protected by the actual malice standard?

Not necessarily. The Court has held that the protection of the *Times* case only applies to statements about official conduct. However, the Court has also stated: "The *New York Times* rule is not rendered inapplicable merely because an official's private reputation, as well as his public reputation, is harmed. The public-official rule protects the paramount public interest in a free flow of information to the people concerning public officials, their servants. To this end, anything which might touch on an official's fitness for office is relevant." Moreover, the Court has declared that a charge of criminal conduct, no matter how remote in time or place, can never be irrelevant to an official's or a candidate's fitness for office when one is applying the actual malice requirement.

What about libel plaintiffs who are not public officials?

We knew you'd ask. In 1967, three years after the *Times* case was decided, the Court extended the protection of its new rule to allegedly libelous statements made about people who were not public officials but were "public figures": a college football coach and an outspoken retired army general. Then, a few years later, the Court also seemed to extend the new rule to libelous statements about people who were neither public officials nor public figures (i.e., "private figures") where the statements concerned matters "of public or general interest." However, in the 1974 *Gertz* case the Court withdrew this protection and rewrote further most of our law of libel.

What happened in *Gertz*?

In *Gertz v. Robert Welch, Inc.*, the Court declared that libel plaintiffs who were not public officials or public figures should not be required to meet the stringent *Times* test to recover for libelous statements made about them—even if the statements concerned matters of public or general interest. However, the Court also ruled that the First Amendment would not tolerate a return to the pre-1964 law where a defamatory statement was presumed to be false and to have caused injury to the subject's reputation. Instead, the Court created a new set of ground rules for libel cases brought by private persons while leaving intact its rules for public officials and public figures.

What was *Gertz* about?

The plaintiff, a practicing lawyer in Chicago, was active in community and professional affairs, had served as an officer of local civic groups and various professional organizations, and had written several books and articles. As a private lawyer, he was retained by the family of a youth killed by a Chicago policeman for the family's lawsuit against the policeman for damages. The defendant was the publisher of "American Opinion," a publication of the John Birch Society. In an article that purported to demonstrate that the prosecution of the policeman was a "frame-up" and part of a Communist campaign to discredit local law-enforcement agencies, Gertz was portrayed as an architect of the frame-up (whose police file took "a big, Irish cop to lift"), a former official of the "Marxist League for Industrial Democracy, originally known as the Intercollegiate Socialist Society, which has advocated the violent seizure of our government," a "Leninist," and a "Communist-fronter," among other charges.

The trial and appellate courts dismissed Gertz's libel suit, concluding that although he was neither a public official nor a public figure, the actual malice test still applied because the defendant's statements about him involved a matter of public interest. They found that Gertz could not show that the defendant published the statements with actual malice, and thus he could not recover for libel.

What did the Supreme Court do?

A lot. It reversed the lower court rulings and ordered a new trial with new rules. The Court agreed that Gertz was not a public official or a public figure but did not agree that the actual malice standard applies to statements about private figures that involve matters of public interest. The Court declined to go back to the pre-1964 libel law, however. It made important rulings on the definition of a public figure, the law governing private figure libel suits, and what kinds of damages a libel plaintiff can recover.

If not actual malice, what standard applies to private figure libel suits?

The Supreme Court held that the First Amendment does not require the stringent actual malice test applicable to public officials and public figures when private figures like Gertz sue because such "private individuals are not only more vulnerable to injury than public officials and public figures; they are also more deserving of recovery."

The Court adopted what it considered a middle ground between pre-1964 law and recent rulings, namely that "so long as they do not impose liability without fault, the States may define for themselves the appropriate standard of liability for a publisher or broadcaster of defamatory falsehood injurious to a private individual." The Court ruled that a private figure must prove at least that the defendant was negligent in making a statement and that the states were free to impose more stringent requirements, including the actual malice test.

How did the Court deal with the public figure issue?

On whether Gertz was a public figure, the Court stated:

> That designation may rest on either of two alternative bases. In some instances an individual may achieve such pervasive fame or notoriety that he becomes a public figure for all purposes and in all contexts. More commonly, an individual voluntarily injects himself or is drawn into a particular public controversy and thereby becomes a public figure for a limited range of issues. In either case such persons assume special prominence in the resolution of public questions.

The Court continued:

> Although [Gertz] was consequently well known in some circles, he had achieved no general fame or notoriety in the community. None of the prospective jurors called at the trial had ever heard of [Gertz] prior to this litigation, and [Gertz] offered no proof that this response was atypical of the local population. We would not lightly assume that a citizen's participation in community and professional affairs rendered him a public figure for all purposes. Absent clear evidence of general fame or notoriety in the community, and pervasive involvement in the affairs of society, an individual should not be deemed a public personality for all aspects of his life. It is preferable to reduce the public figure question to a more meaningful context by looking to the nature and extent of an individual's participation in the particular controversy giving rise to the defamation.

After applying that analysis, the Court concluded: "In this context it is plain that [Gertz] was not a public figure. He plainly did not thrust himself into the vortex of this public issue, nor did he engage the public's attention in an attempt to influence its outcome."

Thus, the law now recognizes two kinds of public figures: (1) the person who is a "public figure for all purposes and in all contexts" and (2) "more commonly," the person who "voluntarily injects himself or is drawn into a particular public controversy and thereby becomes a public figure for a limited range of issues."

What became of the *Gertz* case?

A new trial was finally held. The jury found for Gertz and awarded him $100,000 in compensatory damages and $300,000 in punitive damages. That verdict was affirmed by the federal appellate court in Chicago. Ironically, even at the second trial, Gertz was required by the trial judge to prove actual malice on the part of the defendant since the judge found that such proof was necessary to defeat the defendant's qualified "fair report" privilege.

Who qualifies as an "all-purpose" public figure?

Although the Supreme Court indicated in *Gertz* that all-purpose public figures were relatively rare, the lower courts have found a wide variety of individuals and entities who so qualify, including Clint Eastwood, Johnny Carson, the Holy Spirit Association, Ralph Nader, William F. Buckley, and the Reverend Jerry Falwell. In a number of other libel cases, plaintiffs who are less famous nationally but prominent in their localities have been found to be pervasive public figures. Nevertheless, most libel plaintiffs will not qualify as all-purpose public figures.

Who qualifies as a "vortex" public figure?

Besides those who "thrust" themselves "into the vortex" of public issues, the Court in *Gertz* acknowledged that people could become public figures through no choice of their own. As the Court put it: "Hypothetically, it may be possible for someone to become a public figure through no purposeful action of his own, but the instances of truly involuntary public figures must be exceedingly rare."

In a number of cases since *Gertz* the Supreme Court has proved reluctant to find libel plaintiffs vortex public figures. In *Time, Inc. v. Firestone*, a socialite sued *Time* magazine for its account of her divorce litigation. Although the woman had given a number of press conferences, felt it necessary to employ a clipping service, had her divorce reported in over 100 Florida publications, and was involved in a trial that according to the judge included evidence of sexual escapades "which would have made Dr. Freud's hair curl," the Supreme Court said she did not qualify as a public figure: Since she had no choice but to use the courts in connection with her divorce, such use did not make her a vortex public figure in accounts of the divorce.

The Court reached similar results in two other cases. In *Hutchinson v. Proxmire*, a scientist who received public funds to conduct research on monkeys and behavior patterns found himself the recipient of Senator William Proxmire's "golden fleece" award. When the scientist sued for libel, the defendants claimed he was a public figure. Not so, said the Court. The receipt of public funds, the publication of scholarly articles, and limited access to the media was not enough.

The plaintiff in *Wolston v. Reader's Digest Assn* had failed to appear at grand jury proceedings investigating Soviet intelligence activities in the United States in 1958, although he had been subpoenaed. He later pleaded guilty to contempt, largely because his pregnant wife became hysterical on the witness stand during his contempt trial. At the time, he was mentioned or discussed in at least fifteen news stories. Some thirteen years later, he was listed in a book as "a Soviet agent convicted of contempt charges following espionage indictments." The Court said that he was not a public figure even in 1958, since he "was dragged unwillingly into the controversy." His failure to respond to the grand-jury subpoena, the Court found, resulted not from a desire to draw attention to himself or influence the public on an issue but from his ill health.

Summarizing the gist of the Court's ruling, and casting serious doubt on the likelihood of a person's ever being found an involuntary public figure, Justice Harry Blackmun observed: "The Court seems to hold . . . that a person becomes a limited-issue public figure only if he literally or figuratively 'mounts a rostrum' to advocate a particular view." Justice Blackmun would have limited the inquiry to whether the plaintiff was a public figure when the book was published, which he would have answered in the negative, but the Court as a whole did not address the "passage of time" issue in determining the plaintiff's public figure status. In spite of these rulings, lower courts have not hesitated to find a wide variety of libel plaintiffs vortex public figures, including a worldwide religious movement claiming 5 million adherents, a high school senate president, a former secretary in an urban-renewal agency, the president of a major oil company, a prisoner spokesman for other inmates, a law school dean, an author of a self-help book, anti-nuclear protestors, and a grand-jury foreman. However, Miss Wyoming of the Miss America pageant, the son of the president of a major oil company, an apartment house manager interviewed in a television documentary, an unsalaried police informant, a leading manufacturer of soccer balls, and a country-club tennis pro were all found not to be vortex public figures.

In dealing with this issue, many courts have adopted a two-pronged inquiry: (1) Does the alleged libel arise out of a public controversy (i.e., a "dispute which must, when resolved, affect some segment of the general public other than its immediate participants"; a dispute that "must be more than merely newsworthy . . . must not be an essentially private concern such as a divorce")?; and (2) What was the plaintiff's role in that controversy, including the extent to which the plaintiff's involvement was voluntary, the extent to which the plaintiff had access to the channels of communication to counteract false statements, and the prominence of the plaintiff's role in the controversy?

Can fiction and satire be libelous?

Yes. Some of the most controversial libel judgments have involved works of fiction and satire, which, because of the difference in their nature, will be discussed separately.

In most fiction, by definition, the characters and events are "fictitious"; they are created by their author and are not supposed to be accurate portrayals of actual people and events.

Nevertheless, the courts have held that a person who believes she is depicted and libeled in a work of fiction can sue. A person claiming to have been libeled by a work of fiction (or any other work) must establish that the alleged libel was "of and concerning" her. Although the characters in most works of fiction have names and appearances different from their models in real life, if any, it is possible for a plaintiff to persuade a judge and jury that the fictional portrayal is of and concerning her.

A controversial California case provides a good example. A principal character in the defendant's novel *Touching* was a psychologist named Simon Herford who, among other things, conducted nude marathon therapy groups. The author had attended a nude therapy session conducted by a real Dr. Paul Bindrim. Although the novel's therapist had a different name, physical description, and professional background, Dr. Bindrim claimed to recognize himself in the book and (supported by a few colleagues who testified that they recognized Bindrim in the novel) sued for libel. Although the court ruled that Dr. Bindrim was a public figure and had to prove actual malice, the California appellate court upheld a substantial libel judgment in his favor.

The court's use in *Bindrim* of the actual malice test, which looks to the author's knowledge of falsity, seems anomalous since fiction by definition is "false." Also dubious was the court's reliance on the testimony of a few of Bindrim's colleagues in concluding that the fictional portrayal was "of and concerning" Bindrim. Several courts since *Bindrim* have grappled with this problem and in so doing have alleviated much of the concern among authors and publishers about the implications of *Bindrim.*

In a New York case, a novel based upon the notorious "Son of Sam" murders referred in passing to an unnamed sheriff in a manner suggesting incompetence and perverted sexual proclivities. A sheriff from the same county sued, but an appellate court held that he could not prove the statements referred to him because the book was clearly labeled fiction and described incidents in which he had never participated.

And in another New York case, a female character in a novel dealing with the Vatican was portrayed as a prostitute who engaged in abnormal sexual activity. A former friend of the author's whose first name was the same as the character's sued for libel. An appellate court ruled that a person who knew the plaintiff and who had read the book could not reasonably conclude that the plaintiff was the fictional character since the similarities between the two were "superficial" while the dissimilarities in both manner of living and outlook were "profound." For a plaintiff to recover in such cases, the court declared, "statements made about a character in a fictional work . . . must be so closely akin to the real person claiming to be defamed that a reader of the book, knowing the real person, would have no difficulty linking the two. Superficial similarities are insufficient, as is a common first name."

In the notorious *Pring* case, a multimillion-dollar libel judgment arising out of a satire of the Miss America pageant was overturned by a federal appeals court because the plaintiff failed to prove that the publication contained statements of fact about her. Several similarities between the article's Miss Wyoming and the plaintiff, a former Miss Wyoming, claimed by the author to be coincidental, persuaded the court that the story was "of and concerning" the plaintiff. However, the court further held that "the story must be reasonably understood as describing actual facts about the plaintiff or her actual conduct." And because the allegedly defamatory events about the plaintiff were physically impossible and could not reasonably be believed, the court held that those descriptions must be considered statements of opinion, not fact, and therefore incapable of being libelous.

One more very recent case should be mentioned in this context. The movie *The Wolf of Wall Street* was based on a memoir of one of the principals of a "notorious 'over the counter' brokerage house," which recounted the house's various criminal activities, drug use, patronage of prostitutes, etc. The memoir discussed another principal of the house, Andrew Greene, and his role in some of those activities. The movie claimed to be "based on a true story" but also said that some characters were "composites." In the memoir, Greene is described as "frumpy" with "the worst toupee this side of the Iron Curtain." His actual nickname was "Wigwam," referring to his toupee.

The movie had a principal character who was named Nicky Koskoff, whose nickname was "Rugrat." According to Greene, there were several similarities between him and the movie character. Because the movie depicted "Rugrat" engaging in criminal and other nefarious activities, Greene sued for libel and for invasion of privacy (discussed further below). The federal judge in New York hearing the case dismissed the privacy claim—because Greene's name and likeness were not used in the movie—but upheld for trial the libel claim, rejecting the defendants' argument that the "Rugrat" character was not "of and concerning" Greene. The Court explained: "Given the alleged similarities between Plaintiff and Koskoff, and the public nature of Stratton Oakmont's fraud, Plaintiff has alleged sufficient facts to withstand Defendants' motion to dismiss with respect to the 'of and concerning' element of Plaintiff's libel claim."

Whether the author (and publisher) intended the fictional references to be taken as a reference to the real-life plaintiff or acted in reckless disregard of whether they could reasonably be so taken appears to provide an appropriate test that balances the interests of plaintiffs and the rights of authors and publishers, but this test has not yet become the law. The traditional rules of libel, designed to deal with nonfiction, continue to be applied to fiction, and until special rules for fiction are adopted, writers and publishers of fiction are advised to recognize their potential exposure and take steps before publication to avoid these problems. Disclaimers, changes in details that might suggest real persons, and care to avoid inclusion of derogatory false matter that is unnecessary to the artistic integrity of the work, while not guarantees of nonliability, are mechanisms that should be given consideration.

What about satire?

In satire, real people are placed in fanciful, exaggerated contexts to make a satirical point. There is no question in satire of who is described; the question is whether the exaggerated statements qualify as libel.

Two cases illustrate the problem. After the election of President Nixon in 1968, Los Angeles mayor Sam Yorty, who supported Nixon, let it be known that he was available for a cabinet appointment. Paul Conrad, a political cartoonist for the *Los Angeles Times*, portrayed the likelihood of such an appointment in a cartoon picturing Yorty behind his desk on the telephone while a number of attendants in white coats entered his office. In the caption, Yorty says over the phone, "I've got to go now. . . . I've been appointed Secretary of Defense and the Secret Service men are here." Not amused, Yorty sued for libel, claiming that the cartoon accused him of being mentally unstable.

In the second case, as part of its review of the highlights of the year, a Boston magazine rated a local sportscaster "worst" and said he was "the only newscaster in town who is enrolled in a course for remedial speaking." He sued for libel.

The courts in both cases ruled that the claims of libel could not be sustained. In the Boston case, the Massachusetts Supreme Court declared:

> We conclude that a reader would not reasonably understand the statement that [plaintiff] "is enrolled in a course for remedial speaking" to be an assertion of fact. Taken in context, it can reasonably be understood to suggest that [plaintiff] should have been so enrolled. Even the latter statement may be hyperbolic. The author may have meant only that

[plaintiff's] sports news reading needed improvement. On either of these interpretations, the challenged publication states a critical judgment, an opinion.

However, in another recent case the trial court ruled that whether a satiric reference to the plaintiff was a protected form of humor or a grievous libel had to be determined by a jury after a full-fledged trial:

> Humor, then, may well be a defense to a suit in libel, but the mere assertion that a statement was meant to be funny does not automatically absolve the utterer. Humor is intensely subjective. Blank looks or even active loathing may be engendered by a statement or cartoon that evokes howls of laughter from another. What is amusing or funny in the eyes of one person may be cruel and tasteless to someone else. There is always a thin line between laughter and tears. . . . Thus, the writer resorting to parody must be wary, for his shafts may miss the mark, and be cruel without purpose, inflicting real hurt where only laughter was intended. . . .

> It is difficult for a court to impose its own opinions as to the intent and impact of a purportedly humorous work. . . . Just as questions of what is truth, what is reasonable, or what is obscene are left to the collective judgment of a group of laymen serving on a jury, so the question of whether a particular statement is non-actionable humor or compensable libel should appropriately be left to the judgment of a jury.

As with fiction, legal tests looking to falsity, like the actual malice test, are essentially useless in cases of libel by satire, since satire is intentionally exaggerated and in that sense knowingly "false." Here too, a new legal test is required but has not been fully developed. One appropriate standard might be to consider satire as constitutionally protected expression of opinion that by definition can be neither true nor false. Only in those rare cases where satire could not be considered opinion because of seemingly factual assertions should a court determine whether the author and publisher intended the satire to be taken as fact or acted recklessly about whether it could reasonably be so taken. Until such a test is adopted, the courts may continue to apply a falsity standard in cases where falsity is just about the only issue not in dispute.

Can photographs and works of visual art be libelous?

Yes, although there have been comparatively few cases. In one famous case, an optical illusion in which the plaintiff's genitals appeared to be exposed resulted in a recovery for libel. A more recent case involved a painting titled *The Mugging of the Muse* in which several masked figures were portrayed mugging a female form while cherubs and the like hovered nearby. The plaintiffs, whose faces appeared on the masks, claimed that the painting accused them of being violent criminals. The artist claimed that his painting was an allegorical statement of his opinion that the plaintiffs were enemies of art. A jury sustained the plaintiffs' claims, and the trial judge upheld that verdict. But an appellate court reversed the judgment. The court accepted the jury's finding that the artist intended to, and did, portray the plaintiffs in the painting, and it assumed that a work of art can be libelous. Nonetheless, it held that the libel claim could not be sustained since the painting was clearly allegorical and as such should be considered a non-actionable statement of opinion.

But the fact remains that a person can successfully sue for libel by a work of visual art if he satisfies all the legal requirements discussed in this chapter.

Where can a creator be sued for libel?

In theory at least, libel injury may occur wherever defamatory matter is circulated to persons who know the plaintiff and can be influenced by its publication. A statement published or broadcast in the mass media can cause injury almost anywhere. The "jurisdictional" question is whether circulation of the libel within a given locale (or "forum") has caused injury in that forum and whether the publisher or author's contacts with the forum are sufficient to permit jurisdiction. It is generally held that circulation of a libel in a forum causes injury in the forum. Once actionable injury is established, the question becomes to what extent and on what basis a forum can legitimately reach out to assert jurisdiction over a nonresident. The limits of such jurisdiction are found in constitutional concepts of due process and the First Amendment.

In 1984 the Supreme Court rendered two important decisions dealing with jurisdiction in libel cases. In the *Calder* case, the actress Shirley Jones sued the *National Enquirer* and two of its employees in a state court in California. All of the defendants were Florida residents, and the two employees had extremely limited contacts with California. The Court found that the employees could be sued in California:

> The Due Process clause of the Fourteenth Amendment
> to the United States Constitution permits personal

jurisdiction over a defendant in any state with which the defendant has "certain minimum contacts . . . such that the maintenance of the suit does not offend 'traditional notions of fair play and substantial justice.'" . . . In judging minimum contacts, a court properly focuses on "the relationship among the defendant, the forum, and the litigation."

The allegedly libelous story concerned the California activities of a California resident. It impugned the professionalism of an entertainer whose television career was centered in California. The article was drawn from California sources, and the brunt of the harm, in terms both of respondent's emotional distress and the injury to her professional reputation was suffered in California. In sum, California is the focal point both of the story and of the harm suffered. Jurisdiction over petitioners is therefore proper in California based on the "effects" of their Florida conduct in California.

In the *Keeton* case, a New York resident sued *Hustler* magazine, an Ohio corporation, in federal court in New Hampshire. The plaintiff's only connection with New Hampshire was the circulation there of a different magazine of which she was an editor. *Hustler*'s only connection with that state was the monthly sale there of some 10,000 to 15,000 copies of the magazine. It was clear that the only reason the plaintiff had sued in New Hampshire was that state's four-year statute of limitations for libel.

The Supreme Court found that *Hustler* could be sued in New Hampshire, noting in passing that "false statements of fact harm both the subject of the falsehood and the readers of the statement." The Court concluded: "The victim of a libel, like the victim of any tort, may choose to bring suit in any forum with which the defendant has certain minimum contacts . . . Where, as in this case, [a publisher] has continuously and deliberately exploited the New Hampshire market, it must reasonably anticipate being haled into court there in a libel action based on the contents of its magazine."

As a result of these decisions, a creator who anticipates that her work will be circulated in a given state and that it could cause injury there can also anticipate the possibility of being sued in that state.

If an author or artist is sued in an out-of-state forum and cannot defeat jurisdiction, there is the possibility that she can "remove" the case to a federal court (as opposed to a state court) in the foreign jurisdiction, which may provide a more neutral and hospitable forum for the litigation, or to seek a change of venue to a more convenient forum or in the interests of justice.

How do headlines, captions, and photographs present potential libel problems for the creator?

It is beyond the scope of this book to deal with libel and related problems in news reporting and news publications. But even authors who are not reporters should know that a libel claim may be based not only upon the author's work but its presentation in published form. If headlines, captions, or photographs are added, these can form the basis—alone or in conjunction with the author's material—of a libel or privacy action. In fact, in some jurisdictions defamatory matter in a caption or headline is actionable even if the rest of the story explains away, or supports, the defamatory allegations. In most jurisdictions, however, headlines and captions are read with the rest of the publication and will be actionable based on the meaning of the overall story. If headlines are particularly prominent and so unrelated as to damage the plaintiff's reputation separately, they may be separately actionable. Accordingly, creators should review their material in its final form before publication or secure an indemnification for matter added by the publisher.

Is retraction a meaningful protection from a libel claim?

Not always. Especially in the context of book and magazine publication, retraction protection is often not practically or legally available, or will be of limited assistance in defeating or containing a libel claim. Nonetheless, authors and artists should be aware of this option.

As a matter of common (rather than statutory) law, retraction is often recognized as evidence of an innocent or non-actionable intent. It can support the availability of a claim of privilege or at least limit damages. The law often prevents recovery of punitive damages if a retraction has been made. An effective retraction may also limit the actual harm caused by the initial publication.

There are retraction statutes in several states. They differ widely, but most of them relate mainly or entirely to newspapers, broadcasters, and other "hot news" media. Most book publishers and many magazines could not meet their requirements since time limits for retraction typically range from 48 hours to three weeks. The statute may also require prominent publication (say, on the front page) in a type size the same as or larger than the item retracted, requirements that cannot be met by a book publisher. Still, an offer of a retraction in a letter to the plaintiff, a public announcement, or a correction in a subsequent edition of a book can be made in appropriate circumstances; even if the retraction is technically not in compliance with the rules, and it may be relevant in any ensuing libel litigation.

Are there any other special safeguards available to defendants in libel cases?

Yes. Because of the First Amendment implications inherent in every libel case, the courts, including the Supreme Court, and various state legislatures have established several important safeguards for libel cases that are not necessarily available in other kinds of cases.

In the *Bose* case, the Supreme Court held that appellate courts in libel cases have an obligation to "make an independent examination of the whole record" to be sure that "the judgment [after trial] does not constitute a forbidden intrusion on the field of free expression." As the Court put it:

> The question whether the evidence in the record in a defamation case is of the convincing clarity required to strip the utterance of First Amendment protection is not merely a question for the trier of fact. Judges, as expositors of the Constitution, must independently decide whether the evidence in the record is sufficient to cross the constitutional threshold that bars the entry of any judgment that is not supported by clear and convincing proof of "actual malice."

In the landmark *Anderson v. Liberty Lobby* case, the Supreme Court made an equally important ruling relating to summary judgment in a libel case (where the defendant moves for dismissal based on the established facts and the applicable law, before a trial need be conducted). The Court held that the judge hearing that motion in an actual malice case must evaluate the evidence presented by the plaintiff and decide whether the plaintiff has met his burden of showing by "clear and convincing" admissible evidence that the defendant acted with actual malice. To deny the motion and permit the case to proceed to trial, the trial court must find that "a reasonable jury might find [based on that evidence] that actual malice had been shown with convincing clarity."

And in another major case, the Supreme Court made it clear that the plaintiff in all libel cases, at least where a "media" defendant is involved, has the burden of proving the falsity of the allegedly libelous material.

Finally, many states have enacted "shield laws," which provide under varying circumstances that journalists (which usually includes freelance authors of articles and books) cannot be compelled to disclose their confidential sources, even in the context of a libel suit based on material provided by that source. However, in such cases the courts may take other measures, such as preventing the defendants from claiming they had a reliable source for the material and instructing the jury that it can (but does not have to) infer that there was no source for that material.

Because of the First Amendment aspects of every libel case, the courts have established important protections for defendants. At the same time, the courts have never seriously considered abolishing the right to sue for libel. It is also clear that at least some libel plaintiffs are able to overcome all the protections afforded libel defendants and are able to win substantial libel judgments. The current state of libel law—with elaborate protections for defendants and the possibility of substantial (including million-dollar) judgments for plaintiffs—have led many thoughtful groups and individuals to consider how libel law might be reformed. At the same time, there are those, like President Donald Trump, who believe our libels laws are too protective of defendants and should be "opened up" to make it easier to successfully sue for libel.

What legal remedies are available to a successful libel plaintiff?

Essentially, only money damages. It is generally believed that because of the special threat to the freedoms protected by the First Amendment, the courts may neither issue injunctions against the dissemination of libelous statements nor order a publisher to publish a retraction (or make space available for rebuttal) if the publisher does not wish to.

What kinds of damages can be awarded in libel actions?

Special, general (or compensatory), and punitive damages.

Special damages are out-of-pocket losses that the plaintiff can prove were sustained as a result of the libel; for example, loss of a job, fellowship, or scholarship, or psychiatric or medical expenses. General damages compensate the plaintiff for injuries that are not susceptible to precise calculation—in particular, injury to the plaintiff's reputation. Before the Supreme Court's decisions in the *New York Times* and *Gertz* cases, the law was that once a plaintiff established libel, damage would be presumed without proof. In *Gertz*, however, the Court ruled that presumed damages are inconsistent with the First Amendment. A libel plaintiff (at least in cases involving writers, publishers, or other media) can recover only for proved "actual injury," although the Court went on to observe: "Suffice it to say that actual injury is not limited to out-of-pocket loss. Indeed, the more customary types of actual harm inflicted by defamatory falsehood include impairment of reputation and standing in the community, personal humiliation, and mental anguish and suffering."

And in the *Firestone* case the Supreme Court seemed to indicate that an award of compensatory damages could be sustained constitutionally in the absence of proof of any injury to reputation, but some state courts, including New York appellate courts, have indicated that a libel plaintiff should not recover damages without proving injury to reputation.

Punitive damages are generally only available to address egregious conduct and to serve as a deterrent. In *Gertz* the Supreme Court disapproved the general availability of punitive damages and held that they can be awarded only if the plaintiff proves that the defendant acted with actual malice (i.e., with knowledge that the statement was false or with reckless disregard of its truth or falsity). The Court left open whether punitive damages should be abolished in libel cases. A few states have done so, but the majority continues to allow them.

CLAIMS OF INVASION OF "PRIVACY"

What does the law mean by "privacy"?

There are probably few words that have as many, and as diverse, legal meanings. Privacy has come to mean the right of individuals to decide for themselves (i.e., without government interference) whether to use contraception or have an abortion. The word also refers to the Fourth Amendment right to be free from "unreasonable searches and seizures" by the government. Federal and state privacy statutes are designed to protect the confidentiality of the governmental (and private) records that are maintained on just about all of us.

The word privacy has also (somewhat unfortunately and confusingly) come to refer to four categories of lawsuits, mostly against writers, publishers, and producers, for allegedly invading or violating the "right of privacy" of the claimant. Those four categories are often referred to as "false light," "private facts," "appropriation," and "intrusion."

What is a false light invasion of privacy?

It is similar to libel. The main difference is that although the law of libel is designed to vindicate the subject's reputation, the false light claim is designed to remedy injured feelings. A false light invasion involves "publicity placing a person in a 'false light' in a manner which would be highly offensive to a reasonable person or 'a person of ordinary sensibilities.'" The elements have been succinctly summarized as follows: "The statement must be made public, it must be about the plaintiff, it must be unprivileged, and it must be false. The element of falsity must be proved by the plaintiff and the falsity shown must be substantial and material."

What are some false light invasions?

The Supreme Court has considered two false light cases, which provide useful examples. *Time, Inc. v. Hill* arose from an article in *Life* magazine mentioning the opening of a new play about a family that was held hostage by three escaped convicts. The article indicated that the play was an account of the experiences of a named family some years earlier. The family sued, claiming that its experience was different from that portrayed in the play and that the *Life* article placed the family in a false and embarrassing light.

The Supreme Court, by a 5–4 vote, held that "the factual reporting of newsworthy persons and events is in the public interest and is protected" and that falsity is not enough to defeat that protection. Echoing its landmark *New York Times* libel decision, the Court held that the constitutional protection for speech and press preclude recovery for invasion of privacy to redress false reports of matters of public interest in the absence of proof that the defendant published the report with knowledge of its falsity or in reckless disregard of the truth.

In *Cantrell v. Forest City Publishing Co.*, a woman and her son sued the publisher and reporter of a newspaper article on the impact on their family of the father's death some months before in a publicized bridge collapse. The article purported to reflect face-to-face interviews with the family, but the reporter had had no direct contact with them. The Supreme Court found that there was sufficient evidence to support a finding that the paper and reporter published with actual malice (i.e., knowledge of falsity or reckless disregard of truth or falsity) so a false light recovery could be justified.

Cantrell was decided after the Court ruled in *Gertz* that private figures need not prove actual malice in libel cases. However, since proof of actual malice had been established, the Court did not address whether a false light plaintiff is still required by the First Amendment to satisfy the actual malice test in discussions of matters of "public interest," which is what the Court announced in the *Hill* case.

What is a private facts invasion of privacy?

It has been defined as follows: One who gives publicity to a matter concerning the private life of another is subject to liability to the other for invasion of his privacy if the matter publicized is of a kind that (a) would be highly offensive to a reasonable person and (b) is not of legitimate concern to the public.

Unlike libel and false light claims, which are made about false statements, the essence of this claim is that the statements are true.

Because a private facts invasion must be "not of legitimate concern to the public" and the courts have given broad application to this "newsworthiness" aspect, it is relatively rare that such claims against authors and publishers have prevailed. Most successful cases have been brought against nonmedia defendants such as employers, bankers, and doctors who improperly disclosed embarrassing private facts about the plaintiffs.

There have been exceptions, however, often with plaintiffs who were once notorious but have receded into anonymity. In a celebrated 1931 case, a woman who had been a prostitute and a defendant in a sensational murder case changed her lifestyle, married, and dropped out of sight. Several years later, a movie based on her earlier life was released. The California courts upheld her private facts claim of invasion of privacy.

In a 1971 case, an article about hijacking in *Reader's Digest* mentioned that the plaintiff had stolen a truck in Kentucky and engaged in a gun battle with the police. The article did not indicate that the events had occurred eleven years earlier, after which the plaintiff had moved to California, started a family, and become a respected member of the community. The California courts upheld his claim, stating that while they approved complete reporting about current and past criminal activity, "the identity of the actor in reports of long past crimes usually has little public purpose."

However, many other cases have ruled that "where are they now?" features about once notorious or famous people are "newsworthy" and thus protected. In general, courts will be more sympathetic to plaintiffs' claims if their earlier notoriety was involuntary than if it was of their choosing.

But probably the most famous "private facts" case—ironically prominently reported in virtually every newspaper and magazine—is the 2016 case of *Hulk Hogan v. Gawker*. Hogan, a retired professional wrestler and outspoken radio and television personality—where he freely if not grandiosely discussed his sex life and organs—sued the website Gawker because it published excerpts from a tape showing him having sex with his best friend's wife.

Initially, Hogan sought a preliminary injunction in a Florida federal court. But the judge ruled against him, declaring:

> Plaintiff has failed to satisfy his heavy burden to overcome the presumption that the requested preliminary injunction would be an unconstitutional prior restraint under the First Amendment. Plaintiff's public persona, including the publicity he and his family derived from a television reality show detailing their personal life, his own book describing an affair he had during his marriage, prior reports by other parties of the existence and content of the Video, and Plaintiff's own public discussion of issues relating to his marriage, sex life, and the Video all demonstrate that the Video is a subject of general interest and concern to the community. . . . As such, Defendants' decision to post excerpts of the Video online is appropriately left to editorial discretion, particularly when viewed in connection with a request for a prior restraint.

But then, Hogan took the case to a jury trial in a state court in Florida, and the jury awarded him $140 million, which was upheld by the trial judge and which then led to the bankruptcy and demise of Gawker. And, alas, the bankruptcy meant that the jury's verdict could not be appealed, where many observers believe that verdict would have been overturned.

What is an appropriation invasion of privacy?

Much of it is not really a matter of privacy but the "appropriation" of a person's (often, a celebrity's) name or likeness for commercial benefit without consent or remuneration. Aspects of this branch of privacy law are often referred to as the "right of publicity." Non-celebrities have this right too, but their claims seem more closely related to "privacy" than "publicity" concerns.

The Supreme Court has found that misappropriation or right-of-publicity claims do not inherently violate First Amendment rights. In the leading case, a performer whose act consisted of being shot from a gun prevailed in a suit against a television station that broadcast his act (which took all of fifteen seconds) without consent or compensation. The broadcaster asserted, to no avail, that the performance was newsworthy and therefore protected by the First Amendment.

Occasionally this branch of privacy law is applied (or misapplied) to editorial rather than commercial uses of a name or likeness. However, the law seems clear that appropriation invasion-of-privacy protection does not apply to communications about matters of legitimate public interest, as will be found in most nonfiction newspaper or magazine articles and books. In an important case, the plaintiff's photograph was prominently displayed on the cover of the *New York Times Magazine* to illustrate an article on "the black middle class." He was not named or otherwise referred to in the article, and he disagreed with portions of it. He sued for invasion of privacy under New York's "Right to Privacy" statute, but the New York courts rejected the suit, holding that the publication of his picture was a legitimate editorial use that did not violate any right of privacy recognized in that state. Other courts have found that "fleeting" or "incidental" references to real people in works of fiction (or fictionalized nonfiction) do not violate their privacy or publicity rights.

More difficult problems are presented where real people are portrayed other than fleetingly in substantially fictionalized contexts, including "docudramas." Fictionalized dialogue and events in a biography of a baseball star resulted in a privacy judgment in the star's favor, and some courts have held that satiric performances, parodies, and imitations can violate the right of publicity, even when there is substantial independent editorial content in the material. Elizabeth Taylor once sued to stop an allegedly fictionalized TV movie of her life. However, the case was dropped when the movie was, and it is still not clear how that case would have come out.

Several recent court decisions have further complicated the governing law. In one series of cases, courts have held that the depiction of famous athletes in video games violated their right of publicity, while the federal court of appeals in California rejected the suit by a soldier who claimed that he was the model for the main character in the movie *The Hurt Locker*.

What is an "intrusion invasion of privacy"?

It has been defined as follows: "One who intentionally intrudes, physically or otherwise, upon the solitude or seclusion of another or his private affairs or concerns, is subject to liability to the other for invasion of his privacy, if the intrusion would be highly offensive to a reasonable person." In essence, this refers to wrongful conduct (rather than published work) by writers and media representatives: For example, breaking and entering, surreptitious surveillance, unauthorized physical presence, and the kind of harassing pursuit that some writers and photographers have been known to engage in.

Photographer Ron Galella was found to have violated the right of privacy of Jacqueline Kennedy Onassis by the manner of his pursuit of photographs. Reporters who place a hidden camera and microphone in a private place or who enter a public restaurant or hospital room with cameras rolling and without permission have been found to violate the intrusion privacy right. As a leading commentator has observed, "Crimes and torts committed in news gathering do not ordinarily receive special protection under the First Amendment."

OBSCENITY RISKS

What does the law mean by "obscenity"?

Over the past few decades, there has been an astonishing change in the risks faced by creators who deal in sexual subjects. Just a few decades ago, those creators could justifiably worry about claims that their work was legally "obscene" and legal action, including in criminal proceedings, accusing them of disseminating "obscene"— and therefore criminal—material.

But today, mostly due to the ready availability of explicit sexual material on the Internet, those risks have virtually disappeared. After all, if such materials are so pervasively available for all to see, it is hard to imagine a prosecutor going after similar material in a book, painting, or movie. For that reason, we will only provide here a condensed review of the (ostensibly) applicable law.

The issue of obscenity has confounded the law for centuries. In the United States it has resulted in a clash between advocates of the greatest First Amendment freedom and those who believe that society has the power and duty to suppress at least some sexual expression in the name of public morality.

As a matter of the written law, it can be argued that the forces of suppression have prevailed. Despite the sexual liberation that characterizes our society today, the First Amendment (at least as interpreted by a narrow majority of Supreme Court justices) has been held to permit the enactment and enforcement of state and federal criminal and civil laws against sexually explicit expression, even though suppression of any form of expression is fundamentally inconsistent with the full exercise of First Amendment freedoms. In addition, the mere existence of such laws against obscenity almost inevitably has a "chilling effect" upon other forms of expression that are not obscene but could be prosecuted (and persecuted) in the mistaken belief that they are.

But in another sense it seems clear that creators today have much more freedom of sexual expression than at any time in centuries. Although obscenity laws have been held constitutional, they are permitted to operate only within relatively narrow guidelines. Those limitations, together with the increasing acceptance by large segments of the public of sexually explicit expression and the lack of enthusiasm on the part of most law-enforcement agencies for enforcing obscenity laws, has led to unprecedented freedom.

When obscenity laws are enforced today, the targets are usually the most extreme and distasteful sexual materials: child pornography or pictorial magazines devoted to explicit and often perverse or violent sexual conduct. The era when literary classics such as *Ulysses*, *Lady Chatterley's Lover*, *Fanny Hill*, or the works of the Marquis de Sade could effectively be banned and their authors and publishers prosecuted has passed and probably will not come again. Nonetheless, obscenity laws remain on the books and cannot be ignored by the author or artist whose work includes sexual subjects.

Do obscenity and pornography mean the same thing?

They have somewhat different but related dictionary definitions. Obscenity is the term used most frequently by the law, and it is the term that will be used in this chapter.

For these purposes, obscenity refers to the kind of sexually explicit expression that the Supreme Court has declared not protected by the First Amendment. Courts and legislatures have repeatedly (and almost entirely unsuccessfully) attempted to distinguish the obscene from non-obscene in definitions. But there is no one meaningful legal definition of obscenity today; indeed, the inability of the law to define and limit the legal concept of obscenity effectively is a major reason the continued existence of any obscenity law seriously infringes First Amendment rights.

In addition to works that qualify as obscenity under the current law, the Supreme Court has also held that there are other kinds of (non-obscene) sexually oriented expression that can also be legally regulated and suppressed, including "child pornography" and "indecent" scatological speech when presented on the broadcast media when children are likely to be in the audience. These categories of speech will be discussed later in this chapter.

Why don't obscenity laws violate the First Amendment?

The First Amendment declares that Congress may pass "no law" abridging freedom of speech or of the press. Obscenity laws plainly do abridge those freedoms. Since writings and visual creations that contain sexual themes or explicit sexual depictions seem to be expression entitled to the protections promised by the First Amendment, what happened?

The short answer is that the Supreme Court, the ultimate arbiter of what the Constitution means, has never held that the First Amendment is as absolute as it seems. The Court has proclaimed that certain categories of expression are beyond the protection of the First Amendment, including libel, incitement to riot, and "obscenity." According to prevailing majorities of the Supreme

Court over the past several decades, since obscenity is "without redeeming social value," it is not entitled to First Amendment protection.

How can we distinguish between the obscene and the non-obscene?

This task is made even more difficult by the fact that legal judgments about obscenity involve matters of morality and taste, which are inherently subjective. The elaborate legal formulations of the Supreme Court cannot mask the fundamental impossibility of providing meaningful guidance to authors and artists who deal with sexual themes. What follows is a review of today's legal structure that attempts to define what cannot be defined.

Are there different kinds of obscenity laws?

Yes. Both criminal and civil laws deal with obscenity. Criminal laws typically make it a criminal offense to publish, sell, lend, or otherwise disseminate materials that are legally obscene. Also, exhibition of obscene matter, for example, in motion picture theaters and even in art museums, may be prohibited, and the production (i.e., printing or manufacturing obscene materials) may be proscribed. Some criminal statutes are limited to "commercial" dissemination; others are not.

Creators generally fall within the realm of commercial distribution, which does not depend on whether a profit has been made. Mere possession with the intent to disseminate may be considered a criminal offense. However, private possession of obscene materials for personal use is recognized as constitutionally protected. Advertising the availability of obscenity is also an offense under some statutes, regardless of whether the advertisement is obscene. But with increasing First Amendment protection for "commercial speech," including advertising, these provisions may be constitutionally suspect.

Besides these offenses, which generally involve dissemination or advertising to adults, there are also criminal statutes dealing with distributing or displaying matter that is said to be "harmful to minors" and with creating or disseminating "child pornography," a category of sexually explicit materials subject to a different set of legal standards than obscenity.

Criminal obscenity offenses range from minor misdemeanors to serious felonies, depending upon the state or locality and the circumstances of the offense. Penalties range from fines to prison terms of many years. In addition, in recent decades the federal government and many states enacted "RICO" (racketeer-influenced and corrupt organizations) laws that create extremely harsh penalties for those who commit multiple obscenity violations.

What kinds of civil obscenity laws are there?

Many kinds. And while they do not threaten incarceration, they do provide a range of sanctions that can have an impact on rights of free expression equal to or greater than criminal penalties. They can also place a significant economic burden on the individuals and business interests subject to them. Civil obscenity laws and sanctions include:

- Injunctions against publication, dissemination, or exhibition of materials found to be obscene
- Court orders closing business enterprises that produce, distribute, sell, or display material found to be obscene. Such padlock or nuisance-abatement laws can result in the seizure, forfeiture, or destruction of allegedly obscene materials

- Court orders requiring the "forfeiture" of assets—including books, magazines, movies, and other expressive materials that are not themselves obscene—if they are found to have been acquired in whole or in part as a result of the sale or dissemination of materials that are found obscene
- Licensing schemes providing for prior review and censorship of materials to be exhibited or disseminated
- Civil proceedings to determine obscenity before possible criminal prosecution
- Statutes regulating the display of and access to sexually explicit matter, particularly to children or unconsenting adults, often with criminal penalties for their violation
- Local zoning ordinances intended to limit, concentrate, or disperse sex-oriented businesses

What levels of government can enact and enforce obscenity laws?

All levels: federal, state, and local. Their laws may overlap or be mutually exclusive. The U.S. Constitution, which governs the lawmaking power at all levels of government, has been interpreted by the Supreme Court to permit states and localities to deal with obscenity, but it has also imposed significant limits on this power. Today's constitutional standards even accept the existence of inconsistent laws, so that materials non-obscene in one locality can be obscene in another.

The Constitution permits state and local obscenity laws, but it does not require them. Nonetheless, almost all of the states, and many local governments, have obscenity laws. These laws are often similar, but there are differences, sometimes significant, from state to state and within states. Some states have adopted "statewide standards" or have precluded or preempted local control over obscenity. Although control of obscenity is essentially a local or state matter, there are important federal laws dealing with obscenity. The asserted justification for such laws is to control interstate distribution of obscenity and prevent circumvention of local and state obscenity laws.

Can an idea be obscene?

No. The law today does not permit prosecution of so-called thematic obscenity; indeed, it is generally believed today that under the First Amendment the law may not penalize any idea or opinion, no matter how offensive it may be to lawmakers or the people they represent. The Supreme Court has ruled that the First Amendment protects ideas from attack under the guise of obscenity regulation and has struck down as unconstitutional convictions based upon ideas advocated in a work, even if the work was sexually explicit. For example, the Court struck down a New York statute that permitted censorship of a movie deemed "sacrilegious" and another under which a license for the motion-picture version of *Lady Chatterley's Lover* was denied because it presented adultery as appropriate behavior. In the latter case the Supreme Court declared:

> What New York has done, therefore, is to prevent the exhibition of a motion picture because that picture advocates an idea that adultery under certain circumstances may be proper behavior. Yet the First Amendment's basic guarantee is of freedom to advocate ideas. The State, quite simply, has thus struck at the very heart of constitutionally protected liberty.

It is contended that the State's action was justified because the motion picture attractively portrays a relationship which is contrary to the moral standards, the religious precepts, and the legal code of its citizenry. This argument misconceives what it is that the Constitution protects. Its guarantee is not confined to the expression of ideas that are conventional or shared by a majority. It protects advocacy of the opinion that adultery may sometimes be proper, no less than advocacy of socialism or the single tax. And in the realm of ideas it protects expression which is eloquent no less than that which is unconvincing.

What is the current state of the law?

In 1973 the Supreme Court managed to render its first majority opinion in an obscenity case. However, contrary to the trend of its recent cases, the recommendations of a commission established by President Ronald Reagan, and the urging of many, the Court did not abolish obscenity laws. A new Court majority, composed substantially of Nixon appointees, formulated a new and to a significant extent more regressive definition of obscenity. The new standards were announced in a series of cases generally referred to by the name of one of them, *Miller v. California*. With only limited elaboration since, the *Miller* formulation has remained the prevailing legal standard of obscenity.

How did the *Miller* majority justify the continued suppression of obscenity?

The *Miller* majority reiterated an earlier conclusion that obscene materials are not protected by the First Amendment. It endorsed the asserted "legitimate interest in prohibiting dissemination or exhibition of obscene material when the mode of dissemination carries with it a significant danger of offending the sensibilities of unwilling [adult] recipients or of exposure to juveniles." But it refused to limit the reach of obscenity law to unwilling adults and children. It found that the states have a strong "interest . . . in the quality of life and the total community environment . . . [and in] maintain[ing] a decent society." In addition, it rejected the need for "conclusive proof of a connection between antisocial behavior and obscene material" and thus (implicitly) rejected the findings by the president's commission to the contrary. It held that states could simply "assume" such a connection.

The *Miller* majority expressed confidence that its new formulation of obscenity would provide "sufficiently specific guidelines to isolate 'hard core' pornography from expression protected by the First Amendment" and thus resolve the problems of vagueness, uncertainty, and overbreadth that had plagued the Court, and the law of obscenity, for many years. Finally, the majority found no justification for "sound[ing] the alarm of repression" because of continued enforcement of laws against obscenity. "Public portrayal of hard-core sexual conduct for its own sake, and for the ensuing commercial gain," cannot be equated with "the free and robust exchange of ideas and political debate" that is protected by the First Amendment. "We do not see the harsh hand of censorship of ideas—good or bad, sound or unsound—and 'repression' of political liberty lurking in every state regulation of commercial exploitation of human interest in sex."

And with these considerations in mind, the majority proceeded to rewrite the law of obscenity.

What was the position of the dissenting justices in *Miller?*

Four justices dissented. Perhaps the most significant opinion was that of Justice William J. Brennan, the author of the majority opinion in an earlier case (which first declared that there was such a thing as obscenity that could constitutionally be suppressed). Brennan admitted his past errors: "I am convinced that the approach initiated years ago in *Roth* . . . and culminating in the Court's decision today, cannot bring stability to this area of the law without jeopardizing fundamental First Amendment values." Emphasizing the inherent vagueness and ambiguity of all definitions of obscenity, Brennan declared that the First Amendment "demand[s] that 'sensitive tools' be used to carry out the 'separation of legitimate from illegitimate speech,'" and he "reluctantly conclude[d] that none of the available formulas [of obscenity], including the one announced today, can reduce the vagueness to a tolerable level."

As long as such vagueness exists, Justice Brennan observed, obscenity laws fail to provide constitutionally required "notice" to persons potentially affected, invite "arbitrary and erratic [law] enforcement," and "chill" constitutionally protected expression. Accordingly, Justice Brennan urged the Court to reject the total suppression of obscenity, to protect fundamental First Amendment interests and to prevent the institutional havoc that was the result of sixteen years of disagreement on the Court. He concluded:

> I would hold, therefore, that at least in the absence of distribution to juveniles or obtrusive exposure to unconsenting adults, the First and Fourteenth Amendments prohibit the State and Federal Governments from attempting wholly to suppress sexually oriented materials on the basis of their allegedly

"obscene" contents. Nothing in this approach precludes those governments from taking action to serve what may be strong and legitimate interests through regulation of the manner of distribution of sexually oriented material.

But the majority had one more vote than the dissenters.

What are the elements of the current legal definition of obscenity?

As defined by the *Miller* majority, expressive matter—including writings, photographs, art, dramatic works, motion pictures, and live performances—can be considered legally obscene and therefore constitutionally subject to legal action only if such matter meets of all the following requirements: (1) It must "depict or describe" certain explicit sexual conduct that has been defined as prohibited in applicable state or federal law; (2) The prohibited sexual depictions or descriptions must be "patently offensive" to an "average" person based upon "contemporary community standards"; (3) "Taken as a whole," the material must appeal to the "prurient" interest, again when judged against contemporary community standards; (4) Taken as a whole, the material must also lack "serious" literary, artistic, political, or scientific value.

In formulating these standards, the *Miller* majority expressly indicated that they could be applied constitutionally only to materials that constituted hard-core pornography.

Because the *Miller* standards are now mostly a matter of legal history, and are not actively implemented, we will not parse their specific provisions. But we will note that those standards do not extend to "mere nudity." One commentator articulated the distinction between mere nudity and "lewd exhibition of the genitals," to the extent that any single statement can make sense of inherently subjective and hazy judgments, as follows: "Lewd exhibition of the genitals . . . should be interpreted to include photographs which focus on, exaggerate, or emphasize the genitalia or 'erogenous zones.' It is this exaggeration or 'highlight' on the genitalia which often distinguishes hard-core pornography from mere nudity. Similarly, hard-core pornography often emphasizes suggestive poses or lewdly intertwined bodies, even in the absence of actual sexual activity."

Perhaps because "lewd exhibition of the genitals" is one of the most open-ended *Miller* guidelines, the Court in a subsequent statement on the subject emphasized the need to limit the definition. In discussing the possible overbreadth of a New York child-pornography statute which contained a lewd-exhibition provision, the Court recognized the potential ambiguity and "impermissible application" of the statute, stating: "Nor will we assume that the New York courts will widen the possibly invalid reach of the statute by giving an expansive construction to the proscription on 'lewd exhibition[s] of the genitals.'"

Also, it should be remembered that 25 years after *Miller* the Supreme Court unanimously overturned a Congressional attempt to apply *Miller*-inspired censorship to the Internet (discussed in Chapter 4) and that material that not too long ago would almost certainly have been found subject to *Miller* prosecution is pervasive—and very popular—in cyberspace, thus suggesting that "community standards" now accept such material.

What is child pornography and how does it relate to the general rules of obscenity?

The purpose of so-called "child-pornography" laws is not to limit the dissemination of materials to children (which is the subject of separate laws) but to prevent the use of children in the production of pornographic materials. Thus child pornography is sexually explicit material that displays children engaging in actual (or simulated) sexual activities.

Child pornography laws attempt to proscribe such materials in two ways. First, they impose heavy criminal penalties for the use of children in the creation of sexually explicit (but not necessarily obscene) materials. Second, presenting serious First Amendment concerns, they make it a crime simply to publish or sell such materials, even if the publisher or seller had nothing to do with their production and the materials are not obscene.

In 1981 New York's highest court held that a New York statute that made it a crime to sell such non-obscene materials was unconstitutional. But the next year, in *New York v. Ferber*, the Supreme Court reversed that decision and held that child pornography materials need not be legally obscene to be constitutionally suppressed. In so ruling, the Court expressly created a new exception to First Amendment protection for such non-obscene materials, an exception that does not require the application of *Miller* standards.

It is beyond the scope of this chapter to discuss this at length, but it seems appropriate to note that the Supreme Court has limited the child-pornography exception to visual depictions of actual or simulated sexual activity being performed by children. Written material and visual work not based on actual activity by a minor are not covered by these laws. To the extent that authors and artists do not deal with such matters, they should not be affected by the new exception. However, it is also clear that such laws can affect works of serious value.

What's the law on sexual depictions on television?
A regular viewer of cable television these days will quickly observe that there seems little constraint on the depiction of sexual subjects in that medium. Sex, nudity, profanity, graphic violence—it's

all there. This is because cable networks (like HBO, Showtime, and FX, to name a few) and streaming services (like Netflix and Amazon, among others) are not subject to the federal "indecency" rules that apply to broadcast media. And while those media may decide for themselves to limit certain content—for example, to accommodate advertisers who may not want to be associated with that content—the Federal Communications Commission does not have the power to regulate them.

Unlike cable and streaming media (and, indeed, the entire Internet), broadcast media are subject to FCC (and governmental) oversight and regulation. The Supreme Court ruled in 1978 that the FCC could regulate the showing of sexual content between 6 a.m. and 10 p.m. Currently, there are about 50 broadcast networks, including the major ones like CBS, NBC, ABC, and Fox, as well as noncommercial networks like PBS, religious networks, and Spanish language networks.

Under current law, these networks are prohibited from airing content that is obscene, indecent, and profane. As with all other attempts to regulate such content, these notions can be infuriatingly vague and virtually impossible to implement fairly and intelligently.

The first significant case involved the airing by one of Pacifica Foundation's radio stations of George Carlin's "seven dirty words" monologue. Even though the routine was clearly not obscene under *Miller*—it did not describe sexual activities—the FCC imposed sanctions on the station. Pacifica appealed the fine to the Supreme Court, where a divided court upheld the penalty. The Court explained that "of all forms of communication, broadcasting has the most limited First Amendment protection" because "the broadcast media have established a uniquely pervasive presence in the lives of all Americans." Broadcasts, in the words of the majority, "extend into the privacy of the home and it is impossible completely to avoid those that are patently offensive. Broadcasting, moreover, is uniquely accessible to children."

These two unique characteristics of broadcast—its "pervasive presence" and its "unique accessibility" to children—were combined with the belief that "indecent" speech falls "at the periphery of First Amendment concerns" to justify this expansive approach to government regulation of (even non-obscene) content.

Although the FCC did not immediately pursue broadcast media for so-called "fleeting expletives," this changed after the 2003 broadcast of the Golden Globe Awards when the musician Bono said that it was "really, really fucking brilliant" to get an award. The FCC promptly fined Fox and Fox appealed this ruling. In 2009, the matter came before the Supreme Court, which determined that the FCC had the authority to broaden its policy from banning repeated uses of profane language to banning any such usage; however, the Court did not decide whether the "fleeting indecency" ban was constitutional. On the return of the case to the federal appeals court in New York, that court ruled for Fox on the ground that the FCC's policy on fleeting indecency violated the First Amendment because it was unconstitutionally vague, noting that "the FCC effectively chills speech, because broadcasters have no way of knowing what the FCC will find offensive." And six months later, in January 2011, the same court sided with ABC against the FCC's $1.2 million fine for showing a buttock on *NYPD Blue*.

The FCC petitioned the Supreme Court to review both cases together. But the Court instead declined to address whether the government still had the authority to regulate "indecency" on television and only ruled that the broadcasters had not been given fair notice of the new FCC policy.

Today it is far from clear what can and cannot be said (or shown) on broadcast television. Words that might well have been found "indecent" in the past are pervasive. But it is also undeniable that the broadcast media are far less "free" from government censorship than are such media as cable and the Internet.

In 2013 the FCC asked for public comment on its indecency policies and received more than 100,000 responses, but this did not result in any change in its regulations. But then-chairman Julius Genachowski did direct the agency to focus only on the most egregious complaints. Organizations like The Parents Television Council have pressed for more aggressive indecency regulation and recently filed complaints after an episode of *Scandal*, which contained a steamy sex scene and which aired immediately following the broadcast of *It's the Great Pumpkin, Charlie Brown*. However, the FCC did not punish the network and the story got little attention in the press.

OTHER LEGAL RISKS

What other kinds of claims can be asserted against creators?

Although most of the claims against creators and their publishers assert either libel or invasion of privacy, and often both, other kinds of claims can be brought. The notorious case of *Falwell v. Hustler* provides a good example. *Hustler* magazine published an ad parody that presented the Reverend Jerry Falwell as having had sex with his mother in an outhouse and getting drunk before preaching, among similar assertions. The trial judge dismissed Falwell's privacy claim before trial, and the jury rejected his libel claim, finding that the parody's charges could not be taken as statements of fact about him. However, the jury did uphold Falwell's claim that the parody constituted the "intentional infliction of emotional harm" and awarded him $200,000 in damages.

A unanimous Supreme Court overturned Falwell's victory, holding that the contents of the ad parody could not reasonably be understood as stating facts about Falwell and that therefore the First Amendment precluded recovery, despite the defendant's intention to cause the plaintiff pain and distress. But the Court did leave open, however slightly, the viability of such claims in the future, stating that plaintiffs could recover for the intentional infliction of emotional distress when they can show in addition "that the publication contains a false statement of fact which was made with 'actual malice.'"

Another kind of claim sometimes made against creators arises under the general heading of "unfair competition," which, like the notion of privacy discussed above, actually encompasses a variety of legal theories.

If an author writes a book or a dramatist writes a play or an artist creates an illustration that prominently features a particular person, organization, product, or trademark—for example, the Girl Scouts or the Pillsbury "Doughboy"—the people who own those entities could claim that those works "dilute" the distinctiveness of the entity's name or identity or create "confusion" as to whether they participated in or authorized the creation of those works. It is also possible that the use of someone else's trademark in the title or body of a work could give rise to claims of trademark infringement.

These kinds of claims are usually unsuccessful, since the courts generally believe that those legal theories should be reserved for "commercial" as distinct from "editorial" contexts. Nevertheless, authors and artists who contemplate such uses should probably consider whether such claims might be made.

Finally, authors, publishers, and producers have been sued by people who claim to have been injured because of errors in a book (or other work)—for example, a recipe in a cookbook that calls for 10 tablespoons of chili powder instead of 1 tablespoon, or instructions in a do-it-yourself manual that would result in a serious explosion. Other claims have asserted that people were inspired to imitate something in a book or movie, including acts of physical violence that injured the claimants. In one case the publisher of *Soldier of Fortune* magazine was successfully sued because an alleged "hit man" had advertised his availability in the magazine and was hired through that ad. In general, courts uphold claims based on actual dangerous errors in a work that result in foreseeable injury but reject claims asserting that a victim or a third party might have been "inspired" or "induced" to cause injury because of something in a work.

Who can be sued in these kinds of cases?

The original creator is always directly exposed, much as the driver of a delivery truck is for any accident. The employer of the creator is also exposed, like the employer of the driver. The publisher or broadcaster may also be exposed, even if the creator is a freelance contributor, as might individual editors, producers, and collaborators who participate in the creation of a work.

It occasionally happens that a plaintiff sues the printer of a work, its distributor and retailer, and even the advertisers who have sponsored it. However, because of the Supreme Court's decision in *Gertz* requiring plaintiffs to prove that actionable statements have been published with "fault" by the defendant, it seems unlikely that such tangential defendants will be found liable.

Who bears the costs of these cases?

It depends on what we mean by costs, and on the relationships among the people and entities involved in the publication. "Costs" has at least three meanings. First, there are the physical and emotional costs inevitably incurred in litigation. Second, there are the out-of-pocket costs of defending a lawsuit: lawyers' fees, investigators' expenses, and the like. And third, there may be an award of damages to the plaintiff.

Creators who are sued bear most of the emotional and physical costs. Their work gave rise to the suit, and their reputations and careers may be directly affected. They are most likely to be intimidated and frightened by a lawsuit (including fear of major financial loss) and least likely to be experienced and sophisticated in dealing with such matters. Publishers or other media outlets are probably more experienced in such matters and can take the suit in stride as an inevitable part of their business.

As for out-of-pocket costs, much depends on the relationship between creator and publisher. A newspaper or broadcaster will almost always assume, at no cost to the creator, full responsibility for legal defense. And usually a magazine or book publisher will assume the initial costs of a joint defense with a nonemployee creator, including providing lawyers to represent both. But this does not mean that such protection must be provided or that the publisher will not ultimately seek a contribution from the creator.

Finally, the original creator will almost always be found responsible for some or all of any damages awarded to the plaintiff, although the publisher will usually also be found liable. At least hypothetically, the publisher's insurance will also cover the creator, although, conversely, the creator may be legally obliged to reimburse the publisher for payments made by the publisher relating to the claim.

In practice, however, the creator and publisher will often agree to share the ultimate liability. The publisher can usually afford the payment of damages much better, especially if it is covered by insurance. And it is increasingly common for creators to be covered by insurance, either through the publisher's insurance or through insurance they obtain separately.

Many of these issues can be dealt with in the contract between the creator and publisher (see Chapter 5).

What can a creator do to minimize the risk of a libel, privacy, or other legal claim?

The first rule is to be careful and accurate. But as the Supreme Court has repeatedly recognized, errors are inevitable, as are libel and privacy (and other) suits arising from those errors. Even complete accuracy does not guarantee that no lawsuits will be filed since some plaintiffs will have a different understanding of the truth and others will bring suit for reasons other than the expectation of winning, such as using the suit as a way to deny the charges against them or to harass and intimidate the creator or publisher. Responsible creators should retain the notes and tapes they have compiled in preparing their work, which will enable them to demonstrate in any future litigation that they acted reasonably and without negligence or reckless disregard of the truth. (However, if the notes would disclose a confidential source, there is the countervailing risk that they may have to be produced in litigation.)

If the subject matter of a creator's work suggests the potential of a libel, privacy, or other claim—for example, if the work accuses its subject of criminal or other improper or unpopular activities—many creators and most major publishers and radio and TV stations will have the work reviewed by a libel specialist, usually a lawyer. The specialist should be able to isolate aspects of the work that can lead to legal liability and suggest ways to minimize legal exposure (e.g., by deft rephrasing or careful editing) and to prepare for the potential legal claim. (This is sometimes referred to as "vetting.") Especially if the publisher does not provide such review, the creator concerned about lawsuits should consider getting such a review on her own.

CHAPTER 4

CREATORS' RIGHTS IN CYBERSPACE

When the preceding edition of this book was published, there was (at least for most of us) no such thing as the "Internet," or "websites," or "social media," etc., and thus no need for a chapter devoted to them. But today, no such book would be conceivable without a serious discussion of the rights of creators in cyberspace.

The previous chapters in this book, including those on Copyright, Libel, Privacy, and Obscenity/Indecency, discuss the legal principles and rules that apply generally to creators and their works—as those principles and rules were developed before and without specific reference to the cyber revolution. Building (and relying) on those chapters, this chapter will examine whether and how those fundamental legal principles and rules apply in cyberspace.

COPYRIGHT IN CYBERSPACE

Are the copyright rights I own in my work the same in cyberspace?

Yes, and not quite. All of the exclusive rights generally available to copyright owners—see pages 31–32—also apply in cyberspace.

Thus, for example, except as discussed immediately below, the owner of a literary work, or photograph, or song, etc., has the legal right to pursue as infringements the unauthorized use of those works on the Internet, including on websites and social media.

OK, then, what are the exceptions?

One of the most significant—and troublesome—exceptions involves what is called User Generated Content (UGC). The development of the Internet quickly saw the emergence of numerous websites that featured—that fully displayed for all to see—content that was uploaded to the site by people who were not associated with the site and who were not the copyright owners of those works. For the most part, those sites—think YouTube, Facebook, Twitter, Instagram—had no effective way of knowing whether works uploaded to them were uploaded with or without the authority of their owners. In fact, most of those sites processed those works through computerized programs without human involvement. And this lack of knowledge created a real crisis for contemporary copyright law. By definition, by publicly displaying works without (hypothetically) the authorization of their owners, those sites would be infringing the copyrights protecting those works. But holding the sites strictly liable for infringement under those circumstances would almost certainly preclude such UGC sites from ever launching in the first place. What to do?

So what's now the law for UGC "infringements"?

We thought you'd ask. In 1998, the U.S. Congress enacted the Digital Millennium Copyright Act—commonly referred to as the DMCA—which (among various other provisions) established a whole new legal regime for UGC sites. A full discussion of that entire new regime is beyond the scope of this book. But here are the highlights: A qualifying site (called Internet Service Provider, or ISP) that displays without authority a copyrighted work won't be liable for infringement (called "safe harbor") IF (a) it did not have prior knowledge of (or reason to suspect) the infringing nature of the use; (b) it promptly removed the use upon receipt of a (legally sufficient) "takedown" notice from the owner; and (c) it complied with other requirements for eligibility for "safe harbor" protection.

What should I know about "takedown" notices?

A (sufficient) takedown notice enables a copyright owner to formally demand that an ISP remove content on its site that infringes the owner's copyright. Significantly, unlike other aspects of copyright law—like suing for infringement—the DMCA takedown process does not require the owner to have registered the copyright.

Here are the two most important requirements: (1) You must be the owner of the copyright in question or be an authorized agent or representative of the owner; and (2) You must have a good faith belief that the use is infringing—not authorized and not "fair use" (see discussion of the "Dancing Baby" case below).

OK, then what?

Here are the steps to follow when filing a DMCA takedown notice:

1. Determine the correct recipient. The DMCA makes it a prerequisite for "safe harbor" protection that every ISP identify on the site the person to whom notices should be sent. However, you may have to search for the person on the site: sometimes it's located under "Copyright"; sometimes under "Terms and Conditions." If you can't find it, you can search the U.S. Copyright Office's website for its list of DMCA agents.

2. Many ISPs provide on the site a takedown form that can be filled-in and sent directly. That should be the easiest way to send the notice.

3. If an online form is not provided, you will need to send your notice to the designated agent in the manner the site requires, which may not include email.

4. If you are not using an online form, your notice must comply with the following, which is dictated by the DMCA law itself: Your notice must (a) be in writing (whether hardcopy or digital); (b) signed (whether in writing or by electronic signature) by the copyright owner or agent; (c) identify the original copyrighted work (or works if more than one) you claim was infringed; (d) identify (usually by URL) the infringing material; (e) include contact information so the agent can reach you, if necessary; (f) include a statement that your complaint is made in "good faith"; (g) include a statement that the information in the notice is accurate; and (h) include a statement that you confirm under penalty of perjury that you are the owner or are authorized to act on behalf of the owner of the infringed right.

What should happen next?

Within a few days you should hear from the agent either confirming that the infringement has been taken down or requesting further information. If you don't hear promptly, you should follow-up or just resend your notice. For the most part, ISPs will take down challenged uses in response to proper takedown notices. But remember: The ISP will only take down the specific infringing use you identified, and not any other works—including other versions of the same work—that you did not identify in your notice.

What does the "Dancing Baby" case have to do with takedown notices?

Stephanie Lenz, a doting mother, uploaded to YouTube a 30-second video of her infant son "dancing" to a recording by Prince. The folks who police the unauthorized use of Prince's music sent a takedown notice asserting infringement of the song on the video, which YouTube complied with. But Ms. Lenz claimed that the use was protected as "fair use" and should never have been taken down. She sued Universal Music Corp. for sending an illegal takedown notice, and the case— still not finally resolved—found its way to the U.S. Court of Appeals in California. For the purposes of this book, it should be sufficient to report that the court held that people who send takedown notices must at least consider whether the use in question is legally protected as "fair use," although they are not expected to be copyright experts or to hire a copyright lawyer in deciding "in good faith" to send their notices. ("Fair use" is discussed in Chapter 2.)

How well does the DMCA work in real life?

It works pretty well in protecting UGC sites from liability for copyright infringement, although sites have been found to have forfeited "safe harbor" protection because they failed to comply with one or more of the requirements for that protection. But it probably hasn't worked so well for copyright owners.

How has the DMCA served creators?

First, of course, it places the full burden of policing for infringements on the creator, with no corresponding duty on the sites. The DMCA can only work if the creator locates an infringement—which can sometimes be difficult—and then sends off a sufficient takedown notice. And then, if the site complies, all that will be accomplished is that the specific identified infringement or infringements will be taken down—with no other remedies, like monetary damages, recoverable by the owner. And, alas, that take-down notice will not apply to any other (not specifically identified) infringements— even of the same work—on that site. And, double alas, it is not uncommon for some users to (re)upload infringing works even after one (or more) have been taken down pursuant to the DMCA, thus requiring another round of takedown notices, possibly ad infinitum. Not always a happy outcome for creators wanting to rid the Internet of infringing uses on UGC sites.

Is there any other recourse?

In theory, yes. Although the DMCA protects the sites themselves from liability, no such legal protection is afforded the individual users who uploaded the infringements in the first place. So, if the creator can identify and locate those users—often very difficult, if only because they use pseudonyms and otherwise hide their true identities—and then determines that pursuing claims of infringement against them is worth the bother, the creator could in fact secure some or all of the remedies available to all owners in the case of infringement (see Chapter 2).

Is the DMCA likely to change?

Probably not in any major way, if only because it has become fairly entrenched in the lives of all relevant parties. However, changes in technology—including software enabling an ISP to easily search its entire site for a specific work—may facilitate more wholesale takedowns, and the courts may—as a recent federal appeals court in New York did—strengthen the requirements in the DMCA that ISPs maintain meaningful policies to deal with "repeat infringers" and to act proactively when they should be aware of infringing content on their sites.

How else are my rights different in cyberspace?

Maybe not different, but unique to cyberspace is the phenomenon of "linking." Linking occurs when one party on the Internet—

maybe a website, or someone sending an email, or just posting to a blog—provides a computer-ese "address" where other content can be found, possibly including your copyrighted work. "Clicking" on the link will take the clicker directly to that other source, where the work will be immediately visible on the clicker's computer screen. The law today is clear that the mere act of linking—even to infringing content—is not itself an act of infringement. However, if the party providing the link knows or should know that the work linked-to is infringing—for example, "click here to see stolen photos or text from a not-yet-published book"—the linker could be liable for "contributory infringement."

What's the impact of this "linking is not an infringement" rule?

Potentially significant. For example, if a major (financially responsible, easily findable and sue-able) site links to an infringing copy of your work that is situated on an obscure foreign site, the damage to your copyright has effectively been caused by the linking site but you can only pursue for infringement the foreign site actually providing your work. This is not an especially happy situation.

What about "embedding"?

"Embedding" refers to the phenomenon where a site—by itself linking to another source on the Internet—in effect shows the linked-to work—hypothetically yours—on its own pages, as if it originated there. Indeed, as far as the viewer is concerned, there may be no indication at all that the appearance of your work on that site has been digitally imported—borrowed—from that other site. Frequently, the site "embedding" your work has not itself made a copy of or "stored" your work on its servers. The legal question becomes: Is this "embedding"—this borrowing—of your work on that site an infringement that you can legally pursue?

What's the legal answer to that legal question?

Unlike the situation with linking to another site, which is generally not an infringement, there is no clear legal answer as to embedding. Nevertheless, most (if not all) websites that engage in embedding strongly contend that the practice is like linking and should not be considered infringing. On the other hand, groups representing creators are just as insistent that embedding—directly showing—a copyrighted work is a paradigm case of infringement. (Full disclosure: The authors of this book are currently representing a photographer in litigation claiming that a website's embedding his photograph constitutes an infringement. The outcome of that case could provide needed legal guidance on that legal issue.)

What are the stakes?

Potentially enormous. If websites—as well as all other digital displayers of copyrighted work (e.g., computer screens in airports, highway billboards, and other public places) could freely and legally help themselves to and display through embedding any and every copyrighted work ever created without having to obtain (and pay for) the right to do so, the result would be the obliteration of a major source of income for many creators. By way of example, here's a "hypothetical" from that pending litigation: "It is the seventh game of the World Series and during the 'seventh inning stretch' the people in charge decide—without any authority—to display the world-famous photo of the flag-raising at Ground Zero on 9/11 in full on the Jumbotron, where it is seen by 50,000 people in the stadium and by 100 million people on television. Solely to avoid the (presumably high) license fee that would otherwise be required, it is decided to display the photo through embedding." It remains to be determined by the courts whether or not such displays are actionable infringements.

What about search engines?

Anyone who has used a search engine—Google, Bing, Yahoo!, etc.—looking for pretty much anything quickly finds (upon clicking a search result) full copies of all manner of copyrighted works—articles, entire books, photographs, musical performances, poems, paintings, and so on. Why don't those renditions infringe the copyrights in those works? The not-so-legal answer is that a legal finding of infringement would severely curtail, if not completely devastate, the universally utilized and enormously valuable service those sites provide.

A more legal answer was put forward in a 2006 case in response to (made for the first time) claims that Google committed copyright infringement when it "allowed users to access copies" of copyrighted works "stored . . . on an online repository." The claims were rejected on five separate legal grounds: (1) Because a finding of infringement requires "volitional" action by the alleged infringer, and because Google did not take any such action in collecting and making available to users the copyrighted works in question, it could not as a legal matter have infringed those copyrights; (2) the claimant had granted to Google an "implied license" to reproduce and distribute copies of his works because he knew he could prevent Google's collection of his works and did not; (3) the claimant was "estopped"—precluded by his own conduct—from claiming infringement for the same reason; and (4) Google's collecting and making available to users the works was "fair use" under the Copyright Act. The claims for money damages were also dismissed because Google was protected by "safe harbor" provisions for "system caches" in the DMCA.

After 2006, several other courts—for the same or somewhat different reasons—have also held that search engines do not infringe when they generate and make available the (copyrighted) results of their searches.

What about the "Google Book Project"?

In 2004, Google embarked on a massive project that included the digital scanning of the entirety of literally millions of published books, including books that were fully protected by copyright as well as books that were in the public domain. The purpose was to create a new search engine that would allow searchers to seek and find "snippets" from all those books for free, along with information about the books. (For example, a searcher could enter her own name seeking all references to it in the entire Google scanned library. The result would be a few lines that included that name in all the included books.)

Google neither requested nor obtained permission from the relevant copyright owners. Google fully expected to reap enormous profit from associated advertising, which it would not share with those owners. The Authors Guild and several prominent authors believed the whole project was "massive copyright infringement" at the expense of all the authors of all those books, and they launched a major legal challenge to it. But after ten years of intense litigation, and a court-rejected settlement that would have provided 63 percent of all revenue to the authors, that legal challenge was conclusively rejected.

What was the court's reasoning?

The U.S. Court of Appeals in New York found that Google's massive unauthorized digitizing of the books was non-infringing "fair use." The court explained that the purpose of the copying—to create a searchable database for students, teachers, librarians and others to efficiently identify and locate books of interest to them was, in fair use jargon, "highly transformative." In so finding, the court concluded that the public display of copyrighted text by Google was limited, and that the search results did not "provide a significant market substitute for the protected aspects of the originals." In April 2016, the U.S. Supreme Court denied the Guild's request that it review that decision. ("Fair use" is further discussed in Chapter 2.)

What is CMI, and why is it in this chapter?

"CMI" is shorthand for "Copyright Management Information," which refers to the kind of "information" copyright owners affix to their works to establish, among other things, their authorship and ownership of the works. CMI is commonly affixed, often in metadata, to all kinds of copyrighted works including photographs, musical recordings, videos, fabric designs, paintings and drawings, and books and other literary materials.

Finding a widespread practice on the part of many websites and others to appropriate—to steal—copyrighted works owned by others and in so doing to remove the CMI attached to those works, Congress as part of the 1998 DMCA effectively made the practice illegal. Specifically, Congress established that copyright owners—in addition to suing for infringement—can sue for the intentional removal or alteration of CMI and for the knowing distribution of works with removed or altered CMI. More specifically, in the words of a recent case, "the defendant must both know that the CMI is false, and provide or distribute the false CMI with the intent to induce, enable, facilitate, or conceal infringement." Among other remedies, the law provides for a possible award of statutory damages of not less than $200 or more than $2,500 for each separate violation.

Recent cases, including one in New York where prominent photo agencies in effect falsely claimed as their own photos of an earthquake in Haiti that the photographer uploaded to his Twitter account, have upheld awards of the maximum statutory damages—in addition to (much higher) awards for infringement of the copyrights in those photos.

CREATORS AND SOCIAL MEDIA

Most—possibly all—of us have some relationship with social media—including the major platforms, like Facebook, Twitter, Instagram, as well as any number of other smaller sites. Those relationships may be for purely "personal" reasons and/or for more "professional" purposes. Either way, creators should know the impact those relationships may have on their legal rights as creators.

What are the rules?

To participate in—be a member of—any social media platform, you must first sign up—and agree to the platform's "terms of service." Most of us probably have no idea what those terms provide, and most of us—especially with respect to our creative works—would probably be horrified to learn what we've actually agreed to. Let's start with the easy part.

Let's say you have your own Facebook page, or are active on Twitter, and you post on them—for the viewing of your immediate "friends"—a photograph you've just taken or a poem you've just written or a drawing you just created. You obviously agree to those works being viewed—and maybe downloaded and printed—by the people you know have access to your posts. But who else can see those works, and what can they do with them? While the answer may vary somewhat depending on the specific policies ("terms") of each platform, generally speaking all such platforms provide that your friends—indeed, your legions of followers—may also "share" your content on the same platform on which you posted it, assuming they do so in the way the platform proscribes. For example, "retweeting" on Twitter, and "sharing" on

Facebook. (However, at least on Facebook, you can place limits on who can see what you post.)

What else might the site's terms provide?

Let's say you post some or all of your work on your Facebook page. What have you agreed to? For starters, you grant to Facebook a "license" to host—to display—the work, without having to pay you for that license. Importantly, this does not mean that Facebook owns your work, or that you give up your copyright in it. But, assuming you don't place restrictions on who can access your work—and why would you if you're trying to sell or attract attention to it?—you also give other users of the platform the option to "share" your work. While your business (or profile) name will be attached to the work, you do give up control of where it can be posted. This may not always be consistent with how you'd like your work to be managed, and it's not hard to imagine situations where you might not be happy about some of the places your work may be displayed.

Posting work on Facebook does not give Facebook (or anyone else) the right to exploit your work outside the platform. However, the terms of service you agree to do allow Facebook to permit other (non-Facebook) sites to "embed" your content anywhere they choose, as long as they use specific coding that as a technical matter keeps the content on Facebook's platform. This "embed" exception means that your work—any or all of it—can appear (be seen) on (hypothetically) every other website in the world, as long as the work as a technical matter is not "stored" on those other sites.

The same is true for Twitter: If you post work in a tweet, Twitter has the right to "use, copy, reproduce, process, adapt, modify, publish, transmit, display and distribute" it, which includes allowing other sites to "embed" it so that it appears for all purposes as being shown by those sites. With apologies for what follows, but to best make our point, here's a direct quote from Twitter's Terms of Service:

> By submitting, posting or displaying Content on or through the Services, you grant us a worldwide, nonexclusive, royalty-free license (with the right to sublicense) to use, copy, reproduce, process, adapt, modify, publish, transmit, display and distribute such Content in any and all media or distribution methods (now known or later developed). This license authorizes us to make your Content available to the rest of the world and to let others do the same. You agree that this license includes the right for Twitter to provide, promote, and improve the Services and to make Content submitted to or through the Services available to other companies, organizations or individuals for the syndication, broadcast, distribution, promotion or publication of such Content on other media and services, subject to our terms and conditions for such Content use. Such additional uses by Twitter, or other companies, organizations or individuals, may be made with no compensation paid to you with respect to the Content that you submit, post, transmit or otherwise make available through the Services.

In short, by signing on to Twitter, and posting material to it, you give Twitter almost total control over your work and the ability to do just about anything it wants with it. One legal expert, Callum Sinclair, has said that Twitter's terms, to which every new member must agree, "grant extremely broad rights over your content . . . With these terms [sites like Twitter] are saying 'you own your content, but we can just use it however we want.'" However, it should be noted that the full extent of these terms of service have not as yet been directly tested in court, and one recent case actually limited the claimed breadth of them. In that case, a photographer posted on his Twitter account important photos he took of an earthquake in Haiti. Photo agencies helped themselves to the photos, and argued that Twitter's terms of services allowed them to do so. But the federal court in New York rejected that argument: "Construing the Twitter TOS to provide an unrestrained, third-party license to remove content from Twitter and commercially license that content would be a gross expansion of the terms of the Twitter TOS."

Like the others, Instagram does not claim ownership of any content that you post on its platform. But you do grant Instagram very broad license rights: a nonexclusive, fully paid and royalty-free, transferable, sub-licensable, worldwide license to use content that you post. This license grant means that you have given Instagram the right to use any of your photos for free, for any reason, anywhere in the world. Instagram can also give those rights to a third party. Under Instagram's terms, you must ensure that you own the content that you post or at least have the right to grant Instagram these rights and licenses to the content. You are also responsible to pay any royalties, fees or money owed for the content that you post.

While these terms appear to give Instagram unfettered access to your photos, the co-founder of Instagram recently clarified that it is not Instagram's intention to sell your photos (although he didn't say they can't!). Additionally, as is true with Facebook and Twitter, Instagram only grants third parties the right to share (repost or embed) images through the platforms' proscribed methods—although because Instagram is owned by Facebook, third parties can also post your Instagram work to Facebook. Yet none of this means third parties won't take your images and even profit from them. Recently, as a part of an art fair in New York, the "appropriation artist" Richard Prince displayed without authorization giant screenshots of other people's Instagram photos and sold many of these prints for as much as $100,000. (Prince contends that his "appropriation art" qualifies as "fair use," and some courts have agreed and some have not.)

Does giving credit to the original creator make a difference?

It is a common practice on the Internet for websites that post content from other sources to provide attribution to the content creator. Many people believe if they do this they have protected themselves from potential copyright violation. Yet while providing proper attribution may protect the poster from claims of plagiarism (a nonlegal, mostly academic, species of copying), copyright infringement can take place with or without attribution, and conceivably providing attribution may actually establish that the user knew it didn't have the legal right to use the content in the first place. (Most licenses for the use of a creator's work include a requirement of attribution, if only to reinforce that the work has an owner and who that owner is.)

What is Creative Commons?

Creative Commons is an organization established to facilitate the consented-to use of a creator's work on the Internet by automating the permission process. Creators who register works with Creative Commons choose from a menu of options that set forth the types of permission they may grant to people who want to use their work. The choices depend on such factors as the purpose of the desired use and the fees for the use. After several years of giving creators the option of requiring or not requiring attribution, Creative Commons chose to make attribution an automatic requirement of any Creative Commons license. The reason for this automatic requirement, Creative Commons has said, is that over 97 percent of creators requested attribution as a condition for their licenses.

What about sites that "aggregate" content from other sources?

Many websites, including major ones like Google, Facebook, AOL, and Yahoo!, as well as many others, "aggregate"—meaning take from other (usually original) sources and present to their users content that is presumptively protected by copyright as part of a recapitulation (or "aggregation") of such content. Surprisingly, as of this writing, there is no clear legal understanding as to whether such aggregation constitutes copyright infringement or qualifies as, for example, "fair use." In one recent case, the court held that a commercial site with a "closed" subscriber base that copied and stored AP news articles and then displayed portions of them in response to clients' searches was not analogous to a search engine and was instead an infringing "clipping service." But it remains to be determined how the courts will treat the kinds of "open" and more eclectic aggregators that now thrive in cyberspace.

NON-COPYRIGHT ISSUES IN CYBERSPACE

In 1996, the United States Congress enacted The Communications Decency Act, virtually all of which was addressed to sexual content on the Internet. (See below for a discussion of the fate of those efforts.) But also included in that Act—as Section 230—was a relatively brief provision that had nothing to do with "decency," whatever that term means, and everything to do with how the law would treat numerous legal issues that are presented when content is posted to destinations on the Internet that did not create or send that content. That section declared that "No provider or user of an interactive computer service shall be treated as the publisher or speaker of any information provided by another information content provider" and that "No cause of action may be brought and no liability may be imposed under any state or local law that is inconsistent with this section." This section was enacted in direct response to a state court decision holding the provider of an online message board liable for the defamatory comments of third-party users.

Section 230, as it is commonly called—it is also referred to as the "CDA"—has since been interpreted broadly, giving complete legal immunity to a wide variety of sites that present to their visitors content posted to them by unaffiliated third parties that might otherwise lead to serious legal liability. As one federal appeals court put it, "Section 230 creates a federal immunity to any cause of action that would make service providers liable for information originating with a third party user of the service . . . Lawsuits seeking to hold a service provider liable for its exercise of a publisher's traditional editorial functions such as deciding whether to publish, withdraw, postpone or alter content are barred."

What kinds of claims are covered by Section 230's immunity?

Lots. But first, let's say what's not. Because the immunity provided by Section 230 is limited to "state or local" liability, and because the underlying copyright concern is addressed by the "safe harbor" provisions of the DMCA (discussed above), claims for copyright infringement—a federally created exposure—are not included within Section 230's immunity. But otherwise, Section 230 protects sites from, among others, claims of libel/defamation; invasion of privacy; negligent misrepresentation; interference with business expectancy; breach of contract; intentional nuisance; violations of civil rights; and causing emotional distress. It was held to apply to an alleged violation of a state law that forbids dealers in autographed sports items from misrepresenting those items as authentically autographed. It was also found to extend to unfair competition laws. It was also held to protect a library from being held liable for misuse of public funds, nuisance, and premises liability for providing computers that allowed access to pornography. In a recent case, Section 230 was found to protect a site from claims that its content promoted sex trafficking and prostitution. And, as discussed above, linking to other content—even if that content is legally vulnerable—is fully protected.

When can a site lose Section 230 immunity?

Essentially, Section 230 precludes liability even if the site exercises the usual prerogatives of publishers to select, edit, and delete its (third-party-generated) content. It also applies if the site adds introductions and other editorial matter to that content. However, the site could lose Section 230 immunity if it affirmatively adopts as its own the content in question or if it materially changes that content in a legally significant way. For example, if the site edits the statement "Fred Jones is not a drug dealer" by removing "not," a court might find that that change converts the content to that of the site itself. Similarly, if a site links to a defamatory article with the introductory comment "Click here to read the truth about Fred Jones," and if the clicked-to content is defamatory, that could be found to deprive the site of the Section 230 immunity it would otherwise have.

Is Section 230 universally embraced?

No. Many observers believe it goes too far in protecting websites—including especially those that seem to be taking advantage of the law for less than praiseworthy purposes. A good example can be found in a recent opinion from an influential federal appeals court that (reluctantly) afforded Section 230 immunity to a site that the court clearly thought shouldn't have it. The court concluded:

> The appellants' core argument is that Backpage has tailored its website to make sex trafficking easier. Aided by the amici, the appellants have made a persuasive case for that proposition. But Congress did not sound an uncertain trumpet when it enacted the CDA, and it chose to grant broad protections to Internet publishers. Showing that a website operates through a meretricious business model is not enough to strip away those protections. If the evils that the appellants have identified are deemed to outweigh the First Amendment values that drive the CDA, the remedy is through legislation, not through litigation.

Thus, if changes are to be made to Section 230, they will have to come from Congress, and the prospects for such change in the foreseeable future are probably not great, although legislation to restrict Section 230 was introduced in Congress in 2017.

What is "indecency" in cyberspace?

Virtually everyone who has visited the Internet becomes aware that explicit sexual materials—the kind of material that not too long ago was called "hard core pornography"—are readily available, for free (and for pay), for all (including minors) to see, after just a few clicks on their browsers. Given this country's history of criminalizing such content, how did this happen? The answer is that it took a landmark decision of the U.S. Supreme Court in 1997 to declare that the First Amendment precluded sweeping attempts to criminalize such content on the Internet.

What was the case?

For the stated purpose of protecting children from sexually explicit content in cyberspace, in 1996 Congress enacted the Communication Decency Act (CDA), a collection of new laws that made it a federal crime to present such content on the Internet. More specifically, the CDA criminalized the display "in a manner available to a person under eighteen years of age" of content that was "indecent" or "patently offensive as measured by contemporary community standards" depicting "sexual and excretory activities or organs," etc. Thus, content that would be legal for adults to see would be banned if also accessible to persons under eighteen.

Even before the CDA could take effect, in 1997 the Supreme Court affirmed lower court holdings that the law was unconstitutional and had to be permanently enjoined. In brief, the Court found that the law's operative terms—"indecency" and "patently offensive"—were fatally vague, declaring, "We are persuaded that the CDA lacks the precision that the First Amendment requires when a statute regulates the content of speech. In order to deny minors access to potentially harmful speech, the CDA effectively suppresses a large amount of speech that adults have a constitutional right to receive and to address to one another. That burden on adult speech is unacceptable if less restrictive alternatives would be at least as effective in achieving the legitimate purpose that the statute was enacted to serve." Further, the Court quoted an earlier case that "Regardless of the strength of the government's interest" in protecting children, "the level of discourse reaching a mailbox simply cannot be limited to that which would be suitable for a sandbox."

Have there been further attempts to censor the Internet?

None of the breadth of the CDA, and none that became law. Which explains why the current Internet is essentially completely uncensored, with the free and unlimited availability of content that would no doubt horrify the sponsors of the CDA. But this does not mean that there haven't been more narrow attempts at legislation—and extensive "private" censorship on the part of many major websites.

In 2004, New Jersey passed the nation's first "revenge porn" law. That statute makes it a crime for a person who knows "that he is not licensed or privileged to do so" to nonetheless disclose "any photograph, film, videotape, recording or any other reproduction of the image of another person whose intimate parts are exposed or who is engaged in an act of sexual penetration or sexual contact, unless that person has consented to such disclosure." Since then 33 more states and the District of Columbia have adopted similar nonconsensual-porn laws. (Until recently, getting images removed from the Web was most often accomplished by filing a notice of copyright infringement.)

Privately owned websites have also started to make it easier for victims of this kind of use of the Internet to get images taken down (without having to assert a copyright claim). In 2015 Reddit, Twitter, Facebook, Google, Bing, and Yahoo! all adopted policies against involuntary pornography. Perhaps most significantly, PornHub (a pornography website) recently agreed to take down revenge porn as well. Search engines have also agreed to "de-index" revenge porn, so that when you search for a person's name those images no longer appear. Google explained: "Our philosophy has always been that Search should reflect the whole web. But revenge porn images are intensely personal and emotionally damaging, and serve only to degrade the victims . . . This is a narrow and limited policy, similar to how we treat removal requests for other highly sensitive personal information, such as bank account numbers and signatures."

Apart from "revenge porn," have there been other attempts to control content in cyberspace?

Yes, but they have all been relatively narrow in scope. In 1998 Congress enacted specific provisions to protect the privacy of minors under thirteen accessing the web, including the Children's Online Privacy Protection Act (COPPA), which requires sites to secure parental consent for the collection or use of any personal information of young users. The law also sets out what must be included in a website's privacy policy and when and how the site must seek verifiable consent from a parent or guardian. And in 2000 Congress enacted the Children's Internet Protection Act (CIPA), which requires all K–12 schools that receive federal funding or discounts for Internet access to have an Internet safety policy that addresses (1) access by minors to inappropriate matter on the Internet, (2) the safety and security of minors when using email or other modes of electronic communication, (3) hacking, and (4) the unauthorized disclosure of personal information.

Numerous other "censorship" laws have been proposed by Congress and state legislatures, but groups like the ACLU and other advocates have thwarted those attempts because they violate the First Amendment. Among others, those attempts have included the Cyber Intelligence Sharing and Protection Act (CISPA), which was designed to protect the United States from cyber attacks by making it easier for agencies like the NSA to obtain data from technology companies. (Opponents of the bill said that it essentially gave the government the ability to force companies to turn over data and to even censor the web, in the name of preventing cyber crime.) Another attempt was the Protecting Cyberspace as a National Asset Act (PCNAA), a law that would have given the president emergency powers to take control of and shut down portions of the Internet.

What is the law with regard to hacking?

A brief note about hacking, the unauthorized accessing (and subsequent disclosure) of content in supposedly private computer files. Recently, giant commercial entities like Sony, Yahoo!, and Target, as well as a high official of a 2016 presidential campaign, were successfully hacked. Unfortunately, if you are a victim of such activity, your legal recourse is relatively limited, although suits have been brought claiming the sites were negligent in protecting their content. For example, after Yahoo! revealed that personal information was stolen from at least 500 million accounts, the company was sued by users who claimed the company was grossly negligent in protecting their information. (The lawsuit suggested that the breach might have been prevented had Yahoo! complied with its promise to take user privacy "seriously" and enhanced its security measures.) Similarly two former employees of Sony Pictures filed a class-action suit alleging that the company failed properly to secure sensitive employee information, such as Social Security numbers, birthdates, salary information, and medical information.

Most states have laws that require private or government entities to notify people of security breaches involving personally identifiable information. And most states also have criminal laws that can be invoked against hackers, but it is often difficult to identify and prosecute those responsible. Also, it will often be difficult for these plaintiffs to prove actual harm resulting from the hack, which can significantly impede the prospects for such cases.

What is the "right to be forgotten"?

In May 2014 the European Court of Justice declared that people had a "right to be forgotten," at least on the Internet. The case involved a claim by a Spanish man who wanted Google to remove old content about him that he considered damaging. The Court agreed and (in the E.U., at least) ordered Google to comply with requests that it (and other similar sites) delete "inadequate, irrelevant or no longer relevant" data from its search results. In response, Google now makes available to E.U. residents a form they can use to request that identified content be removed.

Predictably, there have been numerous proposals to adopt a similar "right" in the United States. To date, however, no such right has been recognized, and many believe any governmental order to remove otherwise legal and accurate content would violate this country's strong adherence to the First Amendment freedoms of speech and press. In contrast, Europe has a stronger commitment to "privacy" rights than to free-speech values. But it can be expected that legislative proposals and private lawsuits will continue to seek to create such a "right" here, and it should be remembered that (as discussed above) "revenge porn" laws—a form of the "right to be forgotten"—are now in effect across the United States. Also, California has a limited "right to be forgotten" law that allows minors under eighteen to require the removal from public view of information they provided to websites, social media platforms, and apps, to enable them to prevent their being followed for the rest of their lives by things they posted when they were underage. (Similar laws have also been proposed in other states.)

CHAPTER 5

CONTRACTS INVOLVING CREATIVE PEOPLE

The creator who creates work solely for his own personal enjoyment or fulfillment and has no interest in selling or otherwise disseminating the work probably has no need to read this chapter. All others do, because almost any conceivable arrangement for the transfer, publication, or production of a work involves one or more contracts. Indeed, it is probably true that the contracts entered into by creators will prove at least as important to them as the quality or popularity of their work.

We will first review some of the basic legal principles applicable to all contracts and then examine some of the most common contractual relationships involving creators, including in connection with contracts for publishing, screenwriting, theatrical production, rights acquisition, and the concerns of photographers and visual artists.

CONTRACT OVERVIEW

A contract is a legally enforceable agreement or understanding reached between two or more parties about one or more subjects of interest to them. Contracts are often set forth in writing, but many valid and enforceable contracts are not. In fact, many contracts are not even expressed orally; they are simply understood or "implied" by the conduct of the parties or the established customs of their business.

Not every agreement or understanding constitutes a binding contract. For example, an "agreement" between an author and a publisher that they do not desire to do business with each other would not be a contract. More significantly, a mere "agreement" or "understanding" between that author and publisher that they desire to do business together does not constitute a binding contract. An agreement or understanding must satisfy certain basic legal requirements before it will constitute a binding legal contract.

What are the legal requirements of a binding contract?

If you ask most lawyers, you will get a technically correct but largely incomprehensible response, including such terms as "offer," "acceptance," and "consideration." They will tell you that every contract requires them. However, in real life it is often impossible (and almost always irrelevant) to isolate these three factors.

It is probably more useful to see contracts as agreements where each party commits itself to do something that it was not otherwise obligated to do, where that commitment is acceptable to the other party, and where the law will enforce the commitments or compensate for their breach. The commitments or promises constitute the offer, acceptance, and consideration that the law requires.

For example, if an author agrees to allow publisher A to publish his book but the publisher remains noncommittal, no contract has been reached. If the publisher agrees to publish but the author remains noncommittal, there is still no contract. Only if they agree on publication does a contract exist. Moreover, the major components of the agreement must be discussed and agreed upon before the contract will be enforceable. If the sums to be paid the author are not included in the contract, the courts will almost certainly find it fatally incomplete and incapable of enforcement.

A well-known case illustrates the point. John Cheever's widow entered into a formal written agreement with a publisher for the publication of a book of some of her late husband's stories. The agreement, however, did not specify which stories; an editor was to help assemble and select the stories to he included, presumably with Mrs. Cheever. Mrs. Cheever subsequently wanted to terminate the relationship, and litigation ensued. The Illinois Supreme Court found that the agreement was too vague in too many critical respects to be enforceable:

> The agreement sheds no light on the minimum or maximum number of stories or pages necessary for publication of the collection, nor is there any implicit language from which we can glean the intentions of the parties with respect to this essential contract term. The publishing agreement is similarly silent with respect to who will decide which stories will be included in the collection.

This decision created considerable concern on the part of book publishers, who feared that it could jeopardize many of their existing contracts. At the same time, others proclaimed that the Cheever contract was not typical of most publishing agreements and that the decision posed no such threat. In the ensuing years, there has been no noticeable fallout from that decision.

Who may enter into a contract?

Individuals and business entities such as corporations and partnerships can enter into binding contracts unless the law declares that they do not have the "capacity" to do so. People who are insane or otherwise declared "incompetent" do not have this capacity, and in many states neither do children under a certain age (18 or 21); their contracts have to be approved by a legal guardian or parent. A loosely formed organization such as a local block association or ad hoc committee lacks the capacity to enter into contracts in its own name unless it establishes a more formal structure or members of the group join the contract as parties.

Is there a limit to how many parties can enter into a contract?

Except where the law decrees otherwise (as in the "contract" for marriage), the answer is no. Contracts involving creators often have many parties, including several contributors to a work and several publishers. But most contracts are entered into between two parties. Note that one "contract" can actually contain several separate agreements in the eyes of the law.

Are there contracts the law will refuse to enforce?

Yes. Contracts to commit crimes or otherwise violate the law will not be enforced. Contracts that violate the prevailing "public policy," even though not technically illegal, may also be refused enforcement. For example, in one case an author had entered into a contract with a celebrity; they agreed that the celebrity's name would appear as the author of the book. When the celebrity changed his mind, the author sued to enforce the contract. But the court refused, holding that since the purpose of the contract was to perpetrate a fraud on the public, the contract was unenforceable. (The court was careful to distinguish this situation from the usual agreements among coauthors, collaborators, and even ghostwriters, the validity of which it did not question.)

In recent decades, some politically conservative politicians sought to require the National Endowment for the Arts (NEA), the federal agency established to help fund artistic projects, to include in its grant contracts provisions requiring the recipients not to create certain kinds of work with the funds. At the same time, other political voices sought to continue NEA funding without any restrictions (as was the case previously). For a brief period, recipients of NEA grants were required to sign agreements to the effect that none of works created or presented through the grants could be considered "obscene, including but not limited to depictions of sadomasochism, homoeroticism, the sexual exploitation of children, or individuals engaged in sex acts and which, when taken as a whole, do not have serious literary, artistic, political or scientific value." But that requirement was challenged in court, and ultimately Congress rescinded it and replaced it with a directive that the NEA's chairman "shall ensure that artistic excellence and artistic merit are the criteria by which applications are judged, taking into consideration general standards of decency and respect for the diverse beliefs and values of the American public." That directive has also been challenged as a violation of the First Amendment.

Contracts that are entered into as a result of force or duress will not be enforced, but mere "hard bargaining" will not free a contracting party. If a publisher told an author that if he did not sign the publisher's proposed contract, the publisher would destroy the author's only copy of the manuscript, that would be duress and would lead a court to declare the contract unenforceable. However, if the publisher knew it was the only firm interested in the book and offered the author minuscule financial terms on a take-it-or-leave-it basis, such bargaining, however "unfair" or disadvantageous, would not be duress.

Otherwise, the parties to a contract are free to structure their agreement as they please, no matter how unorthodox, difficult, or "unfair" their agreements may seem. In general, the law will not protect or rescue parties from foolish contracts that meet the basic legal requirements.

When must a contract be in writing to be enforceable?

Whenever the applicable law says so. For example, every state has enacted what is called a "Statute of Frauds." Under these statutes, contracts that cannot by their own terms be fully performed within a single year must be in writing to be enforceable. A contract to hire a collaborator to work on a project for two years or a contract to publish a book not sooner than a year after the contract is signed has to be in writing. Most states also provide that contracts involving (at least) a specified amount of money must be in writing. In addition, the U.S. Copyright Act, as well as other state and federal laws, requires that specified agreements, such as the transfer of a copyright or the grant of an exclusive right in a copyrighted work, be in writing.

Even if the law does not require a contract to be in writing, it is almost always advisable. Memories are unreliable, and it may often be difficult to reconstruct an agreement from the memories of the parties. More important, the exercise of reducing an agreement to writing usually forces the parties to focus on the terms of their agreement and deal with the contingencies that may arise. This can only enhance the effectiveness and enforceability of the contract. To be enforceable, the written contract should contain all the major rights and obligations that compose the agreement.

Is a lawyer necessary for a binding written contract?

Almost always, no. Binding contracts can be quite informal, as in a letter or an email or perhaps a series of letters or emails. It is rare that the law requires that a particular form or particular formalities be used. But the more complicated the contract and the more at stake, the more advisable it is to seek the assistance of a lawyer or similar person who is experienced in drafting such agreements. Such persons can usually anticipate potential problems and help ensure that the agreement is as clear and enforceable as possible.

Although many contracting parties (including most publishers, producers, and galleries), have standard forms that they insist be used in their agreements, the law does not require any particular form. Those parties almost invariably are prepared to modify at least some of the terms of their forms while negotiating an agreement. No one should assume that because a proposed contract is set forth on a printed form, it cannot or should not be challenged or changed. Sometimes each party has her own printed form, and the parties use neither and create a new form.

What happens if the parties to a contract disagree about what it provides or one party claims that the other has breached the contract?

Usually they try to resolve their differences by themselves, perhaps with the help of one or more third parties. This is almost always preferable to taking the matter to court, because contract litigation is usually time-consuming and expensive, and often produces results unsatisfactory to all parties. Indeed, many agreements are providing for various forms of "alternative dispute resolution" (ADR, as it has come to be called), which can be as informal as the two parties' agreeing to meet with a third party mediator to facilitate the parties' reaching their own agreement. More formally, it can involve the appointment of a neutral third party to render a binding or recommended decision.

Arbitration is usually quicker and less expensive than in-court litigation. The parties present their dispute to one or more (often three) arbitrators (often experienced in the industry which is the subject of the contract) who have the power to render a full and final resolution to the dispute. Parties to arbitration may, but are not required to, have lawyers. The advantages of arbitration are economy and efficiency. Disadvantages are that arbitrators are not bound by legal precedents and can render almost any decision they consider appropriate and that a party unhappy with an arbitrator's decision cannot appeal it.

All the parties must agree before a dispute can be submitted to arbitration. As a general rule, the party who can least afford the costs of court litigation will desire arbitration; the party who is better able to afford to litigate will not, although in recent years large corporations have opted to insist on arbitration clauses in many of their contracts, primarily to avoid class actions and (potentially generous) juries. Arbitration clauses are especially appropriate (and common) in collaboration agreements and the like where quickness and economy are important.

How do the courts deal with vague or incomplete contracts?

Often, especially with oral or very casual contracts, the parties fail to anticipate contingencies or leave a provision of the contract so vague that it is essentially meaningless. Suppose a collaborator gets sick and can't work for two months. The vague clause that refers to "incapacitation for a significant period of time" becomes important. If the parties cannot resolve their differences, the courts (or arbitrators) will resolve the differences for them.

The courts will first try to decipher the intentions of the parties. They scour the terms of the agreement for clues. If possible, they resolve the dispute from the terms of the agreement. But if that doesn't work, the courts will examine the surrounding circumstances and if necessary consider the established "customs" or "practices" in the field and be inclined to assume that the parties intended to conform to these customs and practices. Many oral or "handshake" contracts, where the parties don't bother even to express their agreement out loud, will be "construed" or "implied" by the courts using these techniques.

Not every contract can be salvaged this way. Sometimes a provision is so crucial to the agreement and yet so indecipherable that the courts will conclude that there never was an enforceable contract. For example, a publishing agreement that called upon the author to deliver the book "as soon as he was satisfied with it" would probably be found so vague as to be "illusory" and thus unenforceable. This shows how important it is for the parties to be as specific and objective as they can.

How do the courts enforce contracts?

In several ways. First, in appropriate cases, they can issue orders compelling parties to perform their obligations under the contract ("specific performance"), and they can issue injunctions prohibiting parties from engaging in conduct in breach of the contract. Such orders are available, in general, only where the remedy of money damages would not adequately compensate for the breach and where the comparative fairness of the situation (the "equities") justifies the granting of extraordinary relief.

Most of the time, however, the courts will require the breaching party to compensate the non-breaching party with money for the consequences of the breach. Not every breach causes injury; if it doesn't, the non-breaching party is entitled only to a nominal award. Even more important, not every breach causes provable injury. For example, if an author fails to deliver his manuscript as promised or if the publisher fails to publish it as promised, it is likely that the non-breaching party will suffer some injury as a result, but before the courts allow recovery of money damages, the party claiming the injury will be required to prove (and not just speculate or surmise) that the injury was sustained and to offer a rational way to calculate the damages. In the absence of such proof, the non-breaching party may not recover anything.

Finally, depending on how serious the breach is, the courts can declare the contract terminated or keep it in effect and compensate for the breach. If a publisher is two weeks late in making royalty payments or underpays royalties by a small amount, it is unlikely that a court will terminate the contract. But if the publisher refuses to make any royalty payments or is found to have deliberately underpaid royalties by a substantial amount, the outcome may be different.

THE CREATOR-AGENT CONTRACT

People tend to be good at what they're good at and not so good at other things. Creative people are no exception. They may be very good at writing books but not very good at (and not very interested in) doing what is necessary to ensure that a book is published and otherwise disseminated on terms that are fair to the author. Or a screenwriter may have written a great script but have no idea how to get it to the attention of potential producers, so that it remains in the screenwriter's desk drawer. For this reason, many creative people enter into contracts with agents (or representatives).

What does an agent do?

Many things. First, the agent will "represent" (i.e., attempt to sell) the creator's work to appropriate parties (publishers, producers, galleries, etc.). Second, when a sale is made, the agent will handle the negotiation of the terms of the contract. Third, the agent will oversee and collect all payments due the creator and attempt to ensure that the other party is complying fully with all contractual obligations. Fourth, the agent will explore, and often handle, other markets for the work, such as a motion picture or television adaptation of a book. And fifth, a good agent will give a client valuable advice and guidance about the client's work.

What should the agency contract include?

As much of the parties' agreement as possible, preferably in writing. For example, does the relationship apply only to one work by the creator or all the work? Does it cover the world or only parts of it? Does it apply to the representation of the creator's work in all media or only some? Does the agent have the authority to commit the creator? Is the representation to be handled by one agent, or is any individual in the agency authorized to act for the creator? What compensation is the agent entitled to? What expenses should the agent be reimbursed for? What happens if the relationship is terminated?

All these questions, and many more, should be discussed and agreed upon before a creator and an agent enter into a contract. Again, although it is not legally required that the agreement be in writing, simply considering these issues and setting down the parties' resolution of them will help ensure that there will be clarity and communication in the parties' relationship. And unfortunately questions that are not answered at the outset may have to be answered later, when one or both parties may be at a disadvantage.

What if a creator works in more than one medium?

Then it's obviously important to have an agent who also works in more than one medium or at least has cooperating arrangements with other agents who work in the media the first agent does not. An author writing a novel for publication may be represented by a terrific agent in the publishing arena, but that agent may be less effective in handling a rights acquisition agreement for a film based on the novel. In such cases, it would be important for that agent to have a cooperating arrangement with another agent who could properly represent the client's interests. Similarly, if the author wishes to write the screenplay, the agent has to be able to negotiate that contract. Creators wishing to work in more than one medium should ascertain a prospective agent's ability and contacts in those areas.

Does the law impose requirements on the creator-agent relationship?

Yes. The law considers the agent a "fiduciary" of the creator, a person who holds a special position of trust and therefore owes the author full loyalty and honesty. In most contractual relationships, the parties are said to be at "arm's length," but an agent owes a much higher personal duty to the creator. The courts will therefore scrutinize the agent's conduct closely.

Because the relationship is a fiduciary one, the law provides that either party can terminate the relationship at will. However, even after termination, the agent may be entitled to compensation for services already performed or as otherwise agreed to. This can become particularly difficult if a creator discharges his first agent and the new agent begins dealing with the publisher of the creator's previously published works. Disputes can arise on the question of which agent is entitled to the commission on income from those books, the first agent arguing that she made the sale and the second arguing that he is doing the follow-up and maintaining communication with the publisher. However, it is generally understood that the agent who makes the sale is entitled to commissions on the work(s) covered by the sale, at least where the agent is discharged without cause by the creator. If the parties are unable to agree about the aftermath of termination, the courts (or arbitrators) will resolve the question.

Many agents include in their contracts a clause that their relationship with their clients is an "agency coupled with an interest." This gives the agent more rights; for example, the agency cannot be terminated at will. However, the mere declaration of "an agency coupled with an interest" does not suffice to make it one; the law requires that such an agent have an interest in the subject of the agency—for example, a financial investment in the project—other than the right to receive commissions or other compensation. Creators should discuss such a clause if it is proposed and agree on what it is supposed to mean.

COLLABORATION CONTRACTS

Many creative efforts are collaborative. Sometimes the contributions are essentially equal (two people working together to research and write a historical novel or biography), while at other times the contributions may be very different, as where one person provides research or expertise to a playwright for the development of a play. All such collaborations require agreements.

What should a collaboration contract include?

As many specifics as possible, preferably in writing. For example, exactly what is each collaborator promising to do? Are there deadlines? How will disagreements be resolved? Who will have the authority to enter into contracts for the work? Who will own the copyright and other literary property rights in the work? Who will own the physical property? How will expenses be shared? How will earnings be divided? How will credit for the work be determined? What happens if a collaborator fails to fulfill his obligations or becomes incapacitated or dies? What about future works, especially works based on this one? Who will represent the work?

These important questions should be addressed and answered, in writing, at the beginning of the relationship. The entire project can be jeopardized (not to mention the emotional, professional, and financial well-being of the parties) if such questions are left to a time when it may be much harder to reach an amicable agreement.

Does the law impose any provisions on the collaboration relationship?

Some, but not many. Perhaps the most important are the provisions in the U.S. Copyright Act on "joint works."

Section 101 of the Act defines a joint work as "a work prepared by two or more authors with the intention that their contributions be merged into inseparable or interdependent parts of a unitary whole." It is not necessary that the collaborators work together, work simultaneously, or even know each other. The crucial element is whether each contributor prepares her contribution with the knowledge and intention that it will be merged with the contribution of others as "inseparable or interdependent parts of a unitary whole."

Almost all collaborations on a written work, or collaborations between an author and an artist or photographer where the intention is to create a unitary whole, qualify as joint works for copyright purposes. The Copyright Act provides that "the authors [creators] of a joint work are co-owners of copyright in the work." All the co-owners are presumed to own equal interests. Each co-owner is free to use or authorize others to use the work so long as he accounts to the other co-owners for the profits, and each is free to sell or otherwise convey his ownership interest and pass it on to heirs. The consent of all the owners is necessary to convey the entire copyright or grant any exclusive right related to the work.

In the absence of an agreement providing otherwise, the collaborators' rights in the work will be as set forth in the Copyright Act. Many collaboration relationships contemplate different arrangements, which makes it imperative that the collaborators agree on such issues and reduce their agreement to a written contract.

Are there form collaboration contracts?

In 1989, the Dramatists Guild, the professional organization for playwrights and dramatists, promulgated a draft form of collaboration agreement. Particularly because a musical play is often an effort involving more than one individual working in collaboration, the Guild determined that it would be advisable to have a draft for use by its members.

The Guild draft provides that copyright in the created work be jointly owned by all of the collaborators. Each collaborator under the Guild agreement could theoretically enter into agreements for the exploitation of the work, subject to accounting to the other parties. However, it is unlikely that any producer would be willing to acquire rights in a play unless the grant was exclusive, and all the parties would have to agree to grant exclusivity.

THE AUTHOR-PUBLISHER CONTRACT

Except for the rare author who is truly self-published, without the involvement of any other parties, anyone who expects her work to be published must eventually enter into one or more contracts with publishers. These contracts can be extremely important to the author.

Unlike the situation in other media, in the American book publishing world there are no industry-wide minimum terms for the author-publisher agreement. Most major publishers of newspapers, magazines, and books have developed their own standard contract forms. However, as indicated above, authors should not assume that clauses in printed forms cannot be questioned or negotiated and should feel free to question any point in a form agreement they do not understand or agree with. Nevertheless, the use of such forms probably gives the publisher an advantage in negotiations since they put the author in the position of having to seek changes in the form rather than having both parties start negotiations on an equal footing. As in any field, the success an author has in negotiating a contract depends largely on his bargaining power; some authors inevitably have more power than others.

It is not our purpose here to discuss in detail all of the usual provisions of author-publisher contracts. For guidance, an author should consult her literary agent or lawyer. Instead, we will concentrate on the aspects of such contracts that have generated legal precedents or have the most direct legal significance for the author. The provisions of a publishing contract depend in large part on the nature of the work and the publisher.

Freelance articles written for newspapers or magazines involve significantly different considerations than books and can vary widely, from agreements for one-time use only to a blanket work-for-hire agreement. Textbooks are covered by contracts substantially different from contracts for "trade" books (the kind sold in bookstores), and trade book contracts vary, depending on the nature, size, and expense of producing the book. Most of our discussion is concerned with the typical trade book contract, but reference will also be made to other kinds of written work.

What is the essential component of every author-publisher contract?

What is sometimes called the grant of rights. As discussed in Chapter 2, the author of an article, short story, or book begins as the owner of the copyright in the work. As such, the author completely controls the destiny of the work. When an author and a publisher agree on publication, the author agrees to "grant" certain rights in the work to that publisher. The contract should set forth the nature and extent of these rights and the rights the author is not granting to the publisher but "reserving" to himself.

It is common for a publisher of magazine articles and stories to be granted very limited rights, usually the right to publish the work once in a magazine (and perhaps again in a collection or anthology drawn from the magazine). But magazine publishers often seek much broader rights, even all the rights, and the author must negotiate about this.

Books are somewhat different. A publisher's standard contract usually states (before negotiation, anyway) that the author grants all, or almost all, her rights in the book to the publisher and that the publisher is obligated to pay the author specified royalties or other sums for those rights. Such an "all rights" grant would include not only the right to publish the book in English in the United States but also the right to publish it in every language everywhere (and to authorize others to do so); the right to authorize others to base a movie, TV show or series, or stage play on the book; and the right to authorize others to manufacture and sell T-shirts, toys, and other commercial items based on the book or characters in the book. The rights in a book other than the right to publish it in book form are often called "subsidiary rights."

The author (or agent) may not wish to grant all rights to the publisher; he may want to limit the grant to, say, the right to publish the book in the United States (and Canada) and limited subsidiary rights, including the right to authorize others to publish "electronic" versions of the book (e-books) and excerpts from the book and to sell the book through book clubs. In such instances, the author wishes to reserve such other rights as "foreign" rights; motion picture, stage, and television rights; and "merchandising" rights, together with the right to dispose of such rights as the author sees fit.

Most trade book authors today are particularly interested in the form in which their books will he published. Traditionally, trade books were published first in hardcover; then (usually a year later) a paperback edition might be published. In recent years, however, it has become increasingly common for books to be published only in paperback or in simultaneous hardcover and "trade paperback" editions. But the most dramatic change to book publishing in the last decade or so is the advent—and widespread public acceptance of—e-book versions of just about every book published. Virtually every publisher these days will insist on being granted "electronic" (or "digital") rights along with the more traditional print publication rights, and most publishers will also insist on offering financial terms for those rights that many authors and agents consider unfair and inadequate. But, at this point at least, those e-book terms from publishers are essentially non-negotiable.

What should we know about e-books clauses in publishing contracts?

For the purposes of this chapter, there are two categories of e-books: (1) e-book versions of books that are originally published in print form by book publishers; and (2) e-book versions of books that only exist in digital form and that are contracted-for directly by the author.

As mentioned, virtually every book publisher today that enters into a contract with an author insists on being granted the exclusive right to publish, or arrange for the publication of, "electronic" versions of the book. Usually, these clauses provide that the publisher can publish its own e-book version (or versions) of the book (a "direct" grant) and/or "license" another publisher to do so (a "subsidiary" right). Also, most book publishers will insist on total control over all aspects of the e-book version, including whether "enhancements"—music, illustrations, animations, other text, etc.—will be added to the e-version, although many authors/agents will seek to limit the authorized e-book versions to verbatim reproductions of the text of the book.

And what about e-book versions directly arranged by the author?

Not every author can—or chooses to—enter into publishing contracts with traditional trade book publishers. For them, an available alternative is to contract directly with an e-book publisher and/or to simply create their own e-books and market them themselves through websites and social media. The contracts available from e-book publishers can vary widely, and authors should review them carefully to be sure they are getting the full "publication," including marketing, they expect and, just as important, to be sure they are not granting to the publisher more rights—including foreign language and audio, stage and film rights—than they want to or should.

Authors who handle their own e-books won't—at least initially—have contracts to deal with, but that can change if they are approached by agents or established publishers seeking to represent the work or to acquire rights to it. And then the previous discussions about such contracts become relevant. And it should be noted that it has happened, albeit rarely, that a book that starts as a very modestly published e-book gets noticed by a major publisher (and/or film or TV company) and becomes a million-dollar success for the author. But, alas, authors should not expect that to happen for them.

Are there other concerns in the author-publisher contract?

Authors should be as clear as possible about what is and is not being granted to the publisher in the publishing contract. Authors should also understand and be satisfied with the payments the publisher is agreeing to make, including royalty rates on book sales, the author's share of subsidiary-rights income, and the "advance" (a payment trade publishers usually agree to pay before the book is written, much less published, that is "advanced" against royalties which will be due the author from sales of the work after it is published). An unclear contract can mean a messy court case later.

What are the author's obligations under a standard publishing contract?

The author's principal obligation in almost all book contracts and most magazine contracts is to deliver by a specified time a manuscript that the publisher finds "acceptable" or "satisfactory." The most common formulation is that the manuscript must be "satisfactory to the publisher in form and content."

The full legal significance of such clauses is far from clear, and they have been the subject of several important court cases. Traditionally, such clauses have been interpreted to mean that the publisher had virtually unlimited discretion to decide whether the manuscript as delivered was acceptable. Under that approach, if the publisher finds the work unacceptable, it has the right under the contract to declare the contract terminated and require the author to return any advance payments. And the publisher could base that determination solely on its own evaluation of the literary merits or financial prospects of the book. Under that traditional approach, the author was almost completely at the mercy of the publisher's discretion. The only limitation was that the publisher had to act in "good faith," a limitation one federal court found violated in an important case.

The case involved a publishing agreement between Senator Barry Goldwater and Stephen Shadegg, an experienced writer, who were to collaborate on a book of the senator's memoirs, and Harcourt Brace Jovanovich, a major publisher. The contract had the standard "satisfactory to the publisher in form and content" requirement. After seeking but not getting editorial guidance from the publisher, the authors submitted their manuscript. The publisher found the manuscript unacceptable, formally rejected it, and then demanded that the authors return a $65,000 advance. When the authors refused to return that advance, the publisher sued.

After a full trial, the court rejected the publisher's claim in its entirety. With respect to the "satisfactory" clause, the court recognized the "very considerable discretion" the publisher had but then stated:

> It cannot be, however, that the publisher has absolutely unfettered license to act or not to act in any way it wishes and to accept or reject a book for any reason whatever. If this were the case, the publisher could simply make a contract and arbitrarily change its mind and that would be an illusory contract. It is no small thing for an author to enter into a contract with a publisher and be locked in with that publisher and prevented from marketing the book elsewhere.

Before a book can be rejected as "unsatisfactory," the court held, the publisher must undertake certain editorial duties:

> Some reasonable degree of communication with the authors, an interchange with the authors about the specifics of what the publisher desires; about what specific faults are found; what items should be omitted or eliminated; what items should be added; what organizational defects exist, and so forth. If faults are found in the writing style, it seems elementary that there should be discussion and illustrations of what those defects of style are. All of this is necessary in order to allow the author the reasonable opportunity to perform to the satisfaction of the publisher. If this editorial work is not done by the publisher, the result is that the author is misled and, in fact, is virtually prevented from performing under the contract.

The Goldwater case was an extreme example of the publisher's failure to perform. In a similar situation involving the rejection of a manuscript and a dispute over the return of the advance, but one where the publisher did provide editorial services, the publisher was found to have acted in good faith and well within its rights under the clause. "A publisher may, in its discretion, terminate a standard publishing contract, provided that the termination is made in good faith, and that the failure of an author to submit a satisfactory manuscript was not caused by the publisher's bad faith." In another situation, a publisher was held justified in rejecting a fiction manuscript when the agreement called for delivery of a nonfiction manuscript on the subject. In other words, if the publisher renders at least some editorial guidance, its discretion is broad, and most creators will not want to litigate the validity of a publisher's rejection of a manuscript. It is preferable to deal with the possibility of rejection when the contract is made.

Several approaches can be explored. First, the contract can require the publisher to give the author a written statement of defects found in the manuscript and a period of time (e.g., 30 or 60 days) to correct the defects. Second, the contract can attach the outline, proposal, or sample materials the author had already shown the publisher, with a clause added that the book will be acceptable to the publisher if it is in substantial conformity with those materials. Third, the contract can incorporate a clause, proposed by the Authors Guild, stating that the manuscript must be "professionally competent and fit for publication," which the Guild considers an objective criterion compared to the subjectivity of the standard clause. Fourth, the contract can include a provision for arbitration to determine whether the manuscript has been properly rejected. Fifth, the contract can provide that if the publisher rejects the book, the author is obligated only to repay the advance out of the first proceeds received from any other publisher of the book. (This is commonly called a "first proceeds" clause.) Finally, if the author is relying on a particular editor at the publishing company and believes the book may be rejected if the editor leaves the company, a clause can state that the author may terminate the contract if the editor leaves the company before a decision is made on the book.

It may be difficult to persuade a publisher to agree to any of these clauses, but where appropriate the effort should be made.

What are the publisher's obligations?

At least one court has ruled that a publisher is obliged to provide editorial assistance to an author, especially if the author requests it.

A publisher who accepts a manuscript has the obligation to publish the book in good faith. Some publishers' form contracts do not contain such an affirmative obligation; however, the courts would probably construe the contract as requiring the publisher to proceed with publication in good faith since otherwise the contract would be "illusory." Authors should ensure that their contracts contain an affirmative duty to publish, preferably within a stated period (e.g., one year or eighteen months after the book is accepted). Some publishers' contracts actually provide that they may decide not to publish at all. If those provisions remain, authors should insist on the maximum possible payment, including the full advance provided for.

What is meant by the term "publish" is less than clear even in the publishing industry. In one case a paperback licensee began distributing its version before the contract's stated start-date, claiming that what it did was standard practice in the industry.

The trial court found that the term "publication" was undefined in the agreement and that the parties' intentions on this issue were unclear, and it found that the shipment and sale prior to the agreed "pub date" was standard in the industry and not a breach of the agreement.

The federal appeals court disagreed. Although the court held that there were definitions of "publish" other than the one in the Copyright Act, it also held that permitting substantial sales prior to the agreed date would render meaningless the language that the paperback edition would be published "not sooner than" the date set forth in the contract. Thus the appeals court found that by shipping prior to that date, the paperback publisher breached the agreement and was liable to the hardcover publisher for damages.

Another federal decision has elaborated somewhat on the publisher's duty to publish. The author of an unflattering book about the DuPont family sued his publisher (and the DuPont company) because of the way the book was published and promoted. The author claimed that as a result of pressure from the company, the publisher significantly restricted its activities on behalf of the book, thus breaching its contractual duty to publish. The publisher contended that it acted fairly, reasonably, and responsibly in publishing and promoting the book and that all of its actions were taken for legitimate business reasons.

Although the federal appeals court disagreed with the lower court's holding that the publisher had breached the publishing contract, it nevertheless declared that a publisher has an implied contractual duty "to make certain efforts in publishing a book it has accepted," including "a good faith effort to promote the book including a first printing and advertising budget adequate to give the book a reasonable chance of achieving market success in light of the subject matter and likely audience." But once such "reasonable initial promotion activities" are made, "all that is required is a good faith business judgment" about how the book should be handled.

Thus authors have at least one legal precedent if they believe their publishers have failed to publish their books in good faith. But this does not mean that authors can tell their publishers how to publish their books or that the courts will second-guess the day-to-day decisions every publisher makes. Publishers still have (and probably must have) great discretion to decide how much energy and resources to put into each book they publish, and it seems likely that the courts will interfere only if they are persuaded that the publisher acted in bad faith or with no "sound business reason," something that is usually hard to prove.

Authors can attempt to ensure that publishers publish their books vigorously. First, they should seek as large an advance payment of royalties as possible, since publishers often work harder to recoup a large investment, even with a book that disappoints them. Second, authors can try to impose specific obligations on their publishers; for example, to print a specified number of copies in the first printing of the book or to spend a specified sum of money on promoting the book, perhaps including a promotional tour by the author. Such clauses will usually be difficult to obtain, but the effort should be made.

Finally, a publisher is obligated to report sales and other exploitation of the book periodically to the author and to pay the sums due according to that report. Most publishers' form contracts permit the publisher to withhold some royalties as a reserve against returns of books shipped to bookstores; many authors and agents try to negotiate restrictions on these "reserves for returns." They also seek to require the publisher to report the number of copies printed, copies sold at particular discounts, copies returned, and so on, since some publishers provide only the sketchiest information about such matters. It is common for the author to have the right, at the author's expense, to "audit" the publisher's financial records relating to the author's work. Such clauses often provide that if errors to the author's detriment over a specified level (say, 5 percent) are found, the publisher must pay for the audit. Authors should always try to have such clauses included in their publishing contracts.

How are the author's royalties computed?

Generally, on the basis of the number of copies sold. Royalty rates may be negotiated, although with hardcover trade editions there is not much room for maneuvering. Publishers of hardcover trade books will usually offer a sliding scale of royalties such as: 10 percent of the retail price on the first 5,000 books sold, 12.5 percent on the next 5,000 books, and 15 percent on all copies thereafter (i.e., all copies after 10,000). Sometimes in negotiations publishers will improve such offers somewhat. But some publishers will not grant a first-time author a royalty higher than 10 percent, and some established authors are able to insist on a 15 percent royalty from the first sale. With paperback sales, most publishers pay royalties as a percentage of the retail price, but the percentages differ—although a common royalty is 8 percent, with possible step increments.

Some hardcover and some trade-paperback publishers will offer royalties based on the net amounts received by the publisher from sales of the work, rather than royalties based on the retail price. In those situations, the author will receive much less, because discounts and other deductions are made before "net receipts" are determined. In addition, publishers often seek to provide that for a small reprinting of the work, the author's royalty should be substantially reduced, even to half of the regular royalty.

Exploitation of other types of rights granted to the publisher (e.g., licenses to book clubs, licenses of rights to foreign publishers, sale of unbound copies or sheets outside of the United States, direct-mail circulation, and perhaps most important, paperback rights licenses) are computed on a simpler basis, with the author receiving a percentage of the income realized by the publisher for those rights—which percentages usually range from 50 percent to as high as 90 percent, depending on, among other things, the specific rights involved. Finally, the contract will often provide for a reduction of the stated royalty in the event the publisher sells copies of the book at a larger than normal discount to distributors or for certain "special" sales (e.g., sales to a single buyer of a large number of copies, who will use them for gift or promotional purposes) and for retail sales directly from the publisher.

An author's remedies if he successfully proves a publisher's failure to pay royalties depends on the extent of the publisher's failure to pay. Unless there has been an extreme case of nonpayment, an author is not likely to be awarded cancellation of the contract with the rights being returned to him. In one case, there was a bona fide dispute concerning nonpayment of a portion of royalties, and thus the publisher's failure to pay fully did not establish a breach of contract entitling the author to cancellation. However, where the publisher willfully and substantially failed to pay an author two-thirds of the total amount of royalties due from a best-selling book, the breach was held "material" and the author entitled to cancellation.

What happens if a lawsuit is brought against an author because of something published?

First you cry. Then you quickly look up the provisions in your publishing contract that deal with this contingency.

In most publishers' form contracts—indeed, in most agreements for the publication or production of any work—the creator makes many "representations" and "warranties" to the publisher and agrees to "indemnify" the publisher against losses if certain contingencies occur. The creator "represents" that nothing in the book is obscene, libelous, or otherwise illegal; invades anyone's right of privacy; infringes any copyright or other literary property right; causes any injury; or violates anyone's legal rights. The author will reimburse—fully indemnify and "hold harmless" the publisher from—any expense (including its attorneys' fees and any damage award or settlement) incurred as a result of a claim asserted against the book, even if the claim is without merit. Under such clauses, the author can be held responsible for the publisher's expenses even if the author did not breach any representations to the publisher, simply because a claim was asserted.

Many authors and agents consider these provisions unfair, and at least some publishers have come to agree. This is especially true if the publisher has conducted, with the author's full cooperation, a legal review of the book and has declared the book legally suitable for publication. It seems difficult to justify requiring the author to serve as a backup insurer if the publisher's evaluation is wrong.

What can the author propose to ameliorate these concerns?

First, authors and agents can seek to restrict the author's representations to the publisher so that they are made "to the best of his or her knowledge." Second, they can seek to limit the author's obligation to indemnify the publisher to amounts paid pursuant to final court judgments. Third, they can ask the publisher to share equally the costs and payments before (and perhaps even including) a final judgment. Last and perhaps most important, they can demand that the publisher extend its insurance coverage to cover the author for such claims, so that except for the inevitable deductible, the author will be protected under the publisher's insurance.

Such provisions, especially the insurance coverage, are becoming increasingly available. Authors should make every effort to secure this kind of protection.

What about other works by the author?

Most book publishers' form contracts contain two clauses dealing with other works by the author. First they provide in very broad terms that the author agrees not to publish any work that would "tend to compete with, or interfere with the sale of the book" that is the subject of the contract. Second, they usually grant the publisher some form of "option" on the author's next book or books.

Many authors and agents are concerned by standard "competitive works" clauses because they are often so vague that it is almost impossible to know what they mean. Courts have not provided useful guidance. It seems likely that if a case were brought, the courts would interpret the clause narrowly to avoid constricting the author's ability to continue to write and publish. Nevertheless, it is important for authors to attempt to narrow the scope of such clauses when the contract is entered into, perhaps by the deletion of phrases such as "tend to" and by the insertion of words such as "directly" and "significantly" before the word "compete." It may also be appropriate to seek to limit the duration of the clause to a year or two after the book is first published.

Option clauses also trouble many authors and agents. Sometimes they provide that the author is required to submit her next book-length work to the publisher before submitting it to any other publisher and that the publisher has the option to publish the work on the same terms in the present contract. Although such a provision may be grossly unfair to the author, it might well be found to be enforceable since it is specific on all of the necessary terms. It should be resisted as strongly as possible.

Some form contracts state that the publisher has the option to publish the author's next work on "terms to be agreed upon." Such clauses, however, have been held by several courts to be too vague (mere "agreements to agree") and thus unenforceable. But many authors will still try to resist them.

Finally, under some form contracts the author agrees to give the publisher the first opportunity to consider and negotiate for the author's next book and then the right to match any other publisher's offer. These clauses may well also be found enforceable. Authors and agents should decide how vigorously they will oppose them, especially because publishers don't usually relent on them.

What about sequels and revisions?

Publishers of some kinds of books, notably textbooks, usually provide in their form contracts that they will have the right to decide whether sequels or revised editions of the book should be published and the right to have such editions prepared by others if the original author cannot or will not prepare them. Textbook authors should be especially concerned about such provisions and should attempt to limit them. For example, they can ask that the contract require the publisher to give the author the first opportunity to prepare further editions at a specified compensation, or at least the right to approve such editions if they are prepared by others. Also, textbook authors should seek compensation from future editions, even if they do not prepare them. They can also seek the right to have their names removed from future editions if they had nothing to do with them.

Some trade book publishing contracts contain similar provisions, but they are less common and tend to be less important to trade book publishers than they are to textbook publishers. Many trade book authors may choose to resist attempts by their publishers to have such control over subsequent editions. As long as the first contract remains in effect, a revised edition of the original book probably could not be issued by another publisher because it would infringe on the exclusive rights to the book granted to the first publisher. A sequel, however, could be published by another publisher unless the first contract forbids it or a "noncompete" clause is read to prohibit it.

How long do publishing contracts remain in effect?

Most book-publishing contracts remain in effect for the full term of the copyright in the book, the life of the author plus 70 years. However, there are several ways the contract may be terminated earlier.

First, most book-publishing contracts contain "out-of-print" clauses that provide that if the book is out of print (which means there are few or no copies still available for sale), the author can demand that the publisher print additional copies within a specified time. If the publisher fails to do so, the author can terminate the contract and get back all rights previously granted to the publisher. Such clauses are often vague about when a book is out of print; frequently they provide that a book cannot be out of print if there are licenses in effect for the publication of the book by another publisher, even if no such books have been published. Authors and agents often seek to revise standard out-of-print clauses to be as specific and protective of the author's interests as possible. Also, with the advent of e-books and print-on-demand availability, many authors and agents seek to have those editions excluded from the out-of-print definition, since in many cases the publisher can keep those editions available indefinitely.

Many standard publishing contracts provide that if the publisher goes out of business, becomes insolvent, or files for bankruptcy, the contracts are terminated and all rights revert to the author. Although the legal validity of at least the bankruptcy provisions is open to question—because contracts can't override the provisions of bankruptcy law—authors should seek to incorporate as much of this kind of protection as they can.

Finally, as is discussed in Chapter 2, the U.S. Copyright Act provides that after a specified period—such as 35 years—the author can recapture rights previously granted and terminate those grants.

What is "self-publishing"?

Many authors may not be able to find a publisher willing to publish their books—at least on acceptable terms—and some authors choose to forego the traditional author-publisher relationship. For those authors, and especially in the era of e-books, there is now the alternative of "self-publishing."

There are various models. An author can contract with an existing e-book publisher to publish an e-book version of her work. Perhaps the best known of such publishers is Amazon. Alternatively, an author may decide simply to create an e-book version himself and offer it on his own (and other) websites and through social media, etc. Or an author may decide to contract with what is sometimes (snarkily) referred to as a "vanity" publisher.

What is "vanity publishing"?

Vanity or subsidized publishing means that the author pays for the printing and publication of a book. Like the more traditional forms of book publishing in which the publisher bears the costs of publication and is obliged to pay royalties to the author, this kind of publishing depends on the contract between the author and publisher. An author who pays the costs of publication should have a full understanding about the number of copies to be printed, the manner and extent of distribution and promotion, and so on, all of which should be spelled out in a written agreement. Otherwise, authors may find that their publishing contracts are more illusory than real and that they are the only customers for their books.

THE SCREENWRITER'S CONTRACT

As with our discussion of publishing contracts, we will not review in detail all of the terms of the typical screenwriter's agreement, especially since the industry standard—the Writers' Guild of America Theatrical and Television Basic Agreement—runs about 400 pages. We will concentrate on those provisions that are the most significant in negotiations and legal disputes. And while there are some similarities between book publishing and screenwriting contracts, particularly the requirement that the author make certain "representations" and "warranties" about the work and promise certain indemnities, for the most part screenwriting contracts are quite different from their publishing counterparts.

How do screenwriting agreements differ from book-publishing agreements?

The essence of a publishing agreement is the author's grant to the publisher of the right to publish the author's work, with the publisher having relatively little control over the book's content. Not so with the screenwriter—usually, a screenwriter is hired by a producer to write a screenplay, and the producer's control during the writing and over the final product is virtually total. Thus, while a publishing contract is primarily a grant of rights from a copyright owner, a screenwriting contract usually resembles an employment relationship where the producer as employer owns and controls all of the screenwriter's work product.

What kinds of screenwriting contracts are used?

As with publishing, different contracts apply to different kinds of screenwriting work. A television writer's agreement is different from that for a feature film writer.

There are many ways in which a screenwriting contract can arise. At one extreme, a writer might write an original screenplay entirely on his own, "on spec," after which the screenplay is acquired by a producer, and a film is produced from that screenplay. In this instance, the screenplay contract also has elements of the kind of "rights acquisition" contract that is used when a producer acquires the right to produce a movie based on a book. This scenario, however, is quite rare. Moreover, even in the "spec" model, the writer will still likely be "hired" to render further services, including revisions.

At the other extreme, a writer might be hired to write a screenplay based on another work (say a previously published novel written by someone else) to which the producer has obtained (or optioned) the motion picture rights. In this instance, the screenplay may be edited, rewritten, or modified by that writer and others, all at the discretion and direction of the producer, and no movie may ever be made based on the screenplay. This is common. Somewhere in between is the contract for a screenplay based on an original "treatment"—a kind of proposal—written by the writer.

Whatever the circumstances, there is one critical element almost certain to be included in every screenwriting contract: The producer will own—usually as a work-made-for-hire—all the work of the writer and can do pretty much whatever she wants with that work. And that control, together with the fact that the screenwriter herself has virtually no say in what happens to that work, is the critical distinction between screenwriting and book publishing contracts.

A screenwriting contract differs from its publishing counterpart in other ways. Because it is often a contract for material to be written in the future, a screenplay contract will specify what the writer is expected to do, giving particular attention to the types of services to be rendered. Also, a screenplay based on material from another medium is often written when the producer has a limited-time option to acquire the film rights to the underlying work and has not yet exercised that right (because that costs money). Thus the time frame for the performance of a screenwriter's services is critical.

Further, screenwriters can often make much more money (at least in the short term) than their book counterparts because minimum payments for screenwriters are considerably higher than the typical advance paid to most book authors. But, unlike book authors, who can receive ongoing royalties as books are sold, as a practical matter the screenwriter will only receive the payments provided for in the contract. Those payments are due in large measure to an organization known as the WGA.

What is the WGA?

The Writers Guild of America, a labor union for screen, television, and radio writers, was first formed as the Screen Writers Guild in 1933, and it negotiated its first collective bargaining agreement in 1941. As technology advanced, radio and television writers also found protection in what eventually became the WGA. (Technically, there are two separate bodies—the Writers Guild of America East, whose members reside east of the Mississippi River, and the Writers Guild of America West.) The WGA performs many services for its members, including a registration service that establishes the date written material was filed with it, which can be important in a controversy involving when the work in question was written.

Authors writing for the screen receive important contractual support from the WGA, something their counterparts writing for book publication do not have available from any source. The WGA has negotiated standard industry-wide contracts, and an author's compensation on many deals will be described as "WGA minimum" or some multiple of that minimum (i.e., "one and one-half times" the minimum). The WGA agreement also sets forth the terms for another critical contract provision, "credit," and a mechanism for resolving credit disputes. Although the WGA Basic Agreement is a lengthy document, authors interested in screenwriting should take the time to familiarize themselves with it so that they can more effectively evaluate a proposed deal. Copies of the WGA Basic Agreement can be obtained from the Guild.

When is the WGA agreement used?

The WGA agreement applies if (1) a producer is a signatory to the agreement or the writer is a member and (2) the contract (a) is executed in the United States, regardless of where services are performed or (b) services are performed in the United States, regardless of where the contract is executed.

This is how the WGA agreement works: A comprehensive contract is negotiated between representatives of the Motion Picture Association of America (MPAA), to which all studios and other major producers belong, and the networks on the one hand and representatives of the WGA on the other. Once a collective agreement is reached and ratified by the WGA, all MPAA member companies, the networks, and other interested parties sign the agreement, committing themselves to offer no less than its minimum terms in all their writers' contracts. Producers who sign this basic agreement often require a nonmember writer to join the WGA. If there is a conflict between the WGA agreement and a writer's separate agreement, the WGA agreement takes precedence to the extent that the other agreement's terms are less favorable to the writer. However, the WGA agreement is only a minimum agreement; the parties are free to negotiate terms more favorable to the writer.

How does the WGA agreement deal with credit?

Dealing with a writer's credit is one of the key components of the WGA Basic Agreement. Indeed, even though a contract may not be within the WGA's jurisdiction because it was executed outside the United States between a nonsignatory and a nonmember, the parties may still provide that credit will be determined in accordance with the WGA provisions. The WGA agreement provides for a credit arbitration if there is a dispute about a producer's proposed credit for the writer. Sometimes a writer will believe he is entitled to sole screenwriting credit (even though others may have worked on the script), and the producer believes the credit should be shared. Disputes can also arise about the order of names given credit.

This is how the system works: The producer sends notice of its proposed writing credits to all writing participants, together with copies of the final script. If there are no objections, the credits become final. A writer can lodge an objection with the WGA, and the credit determination will promptly be arbitrated by the WGA. There are no reported cases of a credit arbitration being challenged by a WGA member, probably because the agreement provides that no member will be entitled to damages or injunctive relief against the WGA or the production company as a result of the arbitration decision. Among other reasons, decisions as to credit are crucial to screenwriters because credit can have a direct impact on the compensation to be earned by the writer—with, for example, sole credit providing for higher payments than shared credit.

How does the WGA agreement deal with the different stages of writing a screenplay?

The WGA discourages writers from writing scripts on speculation by specifying payment for work done at various stages, or steps, in the screenwriting process.

Although rare, some experienced writers can obtain a "flat" agreement whereby they are paid a flat fee to complete the entire project. But most screenwriters get a "step-deal" that includes a series of options. Under those agreements, a producer can elect at certain stages of the project's development to terminate a writer's involvement in a project or to proceed with that writer. Payment at each stage is a portion of the total payment for services and the rights to be assigned. In recent years, however, some writers have begun to insist (with varying degrees of success) on the opportunity to see a project through a first draft and in some instances even a second draft, and to be paid through that stage.

Most of the writing of a screenplay has to be done in the development period, the period preceding the shooting of the film when critical elements of the production, including the final script, are assembled, budgeted, and scheduled. When the screenplay is based on a book, the development period is generally the duration of the producer's option to acquire the rights. Without a finished screenplay, a film cannot be budgeted. And without an accurate budget, it's difficult to get binding commitments for production funding.

On its way to becoming a finished screenplay, a script may go through some or all of the following stages, called "product forms." The writer may first submit to a producer a first-draft treatment, basically a few pages containing a sketch of the plot and characters. The producer may give the writer specific comments and suggestions for changes, and the writer may then write a first revision of the treatment or, if the requested changes are more substantial, a second-draft treatment. This process may repeat itself, the producer again giving comments and the writer then submitting a second revision or third-draft treatment. At any point, the producer may elect to proceed to the next stage or terminate. The next step is to prepare a screenplay based on the treatment. As with the possible responses to the treatment, the producer will comment on the first-draft screenplay, and those comments will then be incorporated into a first revision or second-draft screenplay (depending again on the extent of the changes), and again the producer may make further comments that require still further revisions or drafts. A rewrite may be necessary. A "polish" is the last step, when the final changes in the screenplay are made.

For scheduling, the contract will likely provide for delivery by the writer of at least the first product form by a specific date or within a specified period after execution of the agreement. It will also provide for a specified period after delivery of each product form when the producer is to read and respond to it, the delivery date for the next product form measured from the conclusion of the preceding reading period. In most cases, a producer will have the right to terminate the agreement after any reading period (although writers are attempting with increasing frequency to insist on the right to write the first and second drafts of a script and be paid for them). Also, a producer often seeks the right to extend the agreement before proceeding to the next product form, giving the producer additional time to consider options or to arrange other aspects of the production before proceeding with the screenplay. But even if a producer obtains such a clause, this right to extend will usually be limited by time or subject to other obligations of the writer.

How is a screenwriter paid for these stages?

The agreement will probably provide for a total amount, to be paid in increments keyed to delivery of each product form. Although a part of that total amount is generally paid on execution of the agreement, most of the compensation is keyed to commencement or delivery of each product form, and any right of the producer to terminate or extend the agreement is contingent upon the producer's paying the sums due for services to date. The writer receives compensation for each product form completed. The WGA requires that 10 percent of the payment for each product form be paid on commencement of that form, although it is more common for a writer to be paid between 25 percent and 50 percent on commencement and the balance on delivery. Moreover, if a producer wishes to skip a form (e.g., omit the second-draft treatment and go directly to a first-draft screenplay) the writer must still be paid all amounts due before beginning that new form.

These payments are part of the fixed compensation to be paid to the writer. The amounts are certain, the only uncertainty being whether the project proceeds with the writer; as long as the writer does the work, she will get the prescribed payment. Again, the WGA fees are the minimum for each stage and for the entire process, and those minimums are keyed to a picture's budget, dependent in large part on whether the picture's budget is more or less than $2 million. These minimums can be increased in negotiations in light of various factors, especially the writer's track record.

What other forms of compensation are available?

In addition to the fixed compensation approach, screenwriting agreements often provide for bonus, deferred, and contingent payments. The possibility and amount of a bonus often depends upon the credit (e.g., if the writer receives sole credit, a bonus may be paid). The bonus is often 25 percent to 50 percent of the fixed compensation. There may also be a bonus if the writer receives shared credit, although the amount of the bonus will be smaller. Deferred payments are usually preferred by producers of low budget, often independently financed projects. Let's say a producer can raise sufficient funding from private investors (i.e., not a studio) to produce a "bare bones" film, but without the "right" talent for the project. To attract that talent to the project, the producer may promise specific percentages of the film's future earnings. If a writer is eager to be involved in a project, he may agree to participate for less money up front (i.e., on completion of the various product forms) for the possibility of more later, after the project starts earning money (although not necessarily profits).

Any such provisions should be specified with care in the contract. For example, although a deferred payment is often made after repayment to investors of their investments and before a distribution of net profits, such payments are sometimes made, at one extreme, prior to repayment to investors and, at the other extreme, after investors (or other participants) have not only been repaid their investments but also received some profits. Also, since deferred payments are often paid pro rata with other participants (which means that all deferred payments are totaled and each participant gets his proportionate share of each payment made), it is important to put limits on deferred payments to others or at least be aware of them. Otherwise the amount paid to the writer in comparison with what's paid to other recipients of deferred payments may not be adequate. The ultimate risk with the deferred payment approach is that the production won't be distributed or that not enough income will come in to reach the point where deferred payments are to be made.

What are contingent payments?

The contingent payment is a participation in "profits." The most successful writers can sometimes negotiate a small participation, usually no more than 1 or 2 percent, of the film's gross profits, the amounts received from distribution of the picture, less only certain limited deductions. If a writer is fortunate enough to obtain a gross participation, she may actually see some payments. This is not the case for most of their less renowned colleagues, who are unable to command a gross-profits participation. Many writers will receive some participation, usually between 2.5 percent and 5 percent, of "net profits," although it is a rare film that generates any net profits. To calculate net profits, there must be deducted from the gross (i.e., the total income received from the distribution and exploitation of a film) all deferred payments for talent, production recoupment, distribution fees, distribution expenses, and assorted other items.

There are then two principal types of net profits that may be distributed. Writers prefer a participation based on "100 percent of net profits"; producers prefer to offer a participation in "producer's net profits" because the producer's net is what's left after participants in 100 percent of net profits have been paid. But even with 100 percent of net profits, most writers should not expect to see any real participation; net profit definitions generally are exceptionally long, confusing, complicated, and seemingly designed by the producer to make sure there are none.

A good example is the "Art Buchwald" case, which received international attention in the late 1980s and which opened the door to such challenges. The author and columnist Art Buchwald sold to Paramount Pictures an 8-page treatment titled "King for a Day" about an African king, stranded penniless in the United States, who falls in love with a young woman. Although Paramount told Buchwald that it had no interest in producing a movie based on that treatment, Buchwald claimed that Paramount's subsequent hit film *Coming to America*, starring Eddie Murphy, was based on his work. Buchwald sued Paramount, claiming breach of the provision in his treatment contract that he would be paid if Paramount produced a motion picture "based upon [his] work." The trial court agreed that *Coming to America* was "based upon" Buchwald's treatment and found that under his contract with Paramount, Buchwald was entitled to a percentage of the film's "net profits," if any. Even though the film earned almost $300 million at the box office, Paramount contended that no net profits had been earned under the applicable net profits definition. In fact, Paramount claimed, the film was still millions in the red. As noted in a contemporary article, "The most important thing to know about 'net profit' participation definitions and formulas in the motion picture industry is that they have little to do with profits."

Profit participations in the motion picture industry are best characterized as supplemental contingent compensation based upon cash actually "received" by the studio ("gross receipts" as defined in the particular participation agreement) less certain deductions for certain fees that are typically calculated as a percentage of gross receipts and the direct and indirect cost of making the motion picture.

Since a typical net profits definition, like Buchwald's, can go on for more than 25 pages of that kind of doubletalk, it's small wonder that producers rarely declare that net profits have been realized, even for the most successful films. Significantly, the judge in the Buchwald case declared that several parts of Paramount's net profits definition—which was similar to that of much of the industry—were "unconscionable" (i.e., so unfair that the court would refuse to enforce them).

What does the producer get for his payments to the screenwriter?

Plenty. In fact, with one important exception, noted below, the producer gets the right to do whatever the producer wants with the material created. The writer often has to sign a certificate confirming and conveying ownership to the producer. The producer has the right to modify the writer's work without the writer's permission. The producer can even merge the writer's work with material written by others. The producer can generally use the work in any and all media (now known or hereafter created) throughout the universe. The writer specifically waives any rights of *droit moral* (discussed in Chapter 2).

The sole limitation on the rights conveyed to the producer is a screenplay written from scratch, from an independent creative idea not based on material from another source. In such cases, the WGA Basic Agreement provides that the writer may be entitled to "Separation of Rights," which means that writer may be entitled to certain publication, dramatic, and sequel rights in the original material. Under the WGA agreement, the producer can acquire the separated rights from the writer for additional payment, although such an acquisition should be specifically discussed and included in the agreement; it is not deemed included in the grant of rights to the producer, even if the payment for the writer's services exceeded WGA minimums. However, most producers include a separate grant of separated rights in their form agreements, and in such cases the writer will be deemed to have granted those rights unless the clause is removed or modified.

Does the original screenwriter benefit if there's a sequel or a television series based on the film?

Yes. A typical screenwriter's contract provides that for a sequel (e.g., *Friday the 13th Part 700*), the original writer is entitled to receive stated payments. The WGA minimum payment is 25 percent of the original compensation, although 33⅓ percent to 50 percent is more typical. The same is true of a remake of the original film, even if it has a different title. The writer may also want to provide in the agreement that he will have the right to write the sequel or remake. If agreeable to any such provision, the producer will usually try to limit it to a right of first negotiation (which means the producer has to negotiate in good faith with the writer before approaching another writer) and to limit the provision to a specified period, often between 7 and 10 years from the first release of the initial picture. The original writer will also receive a royalty for each episode of a television series based on an original screenplay. Again, the writer may also seek a right to participate in the creation of the series, although that effort is usually unsuccessful.

THE PLAYWRIGHT'S AGREEMENT

A playwright's agreement with a producer resembles in some ways the author-publisher agreement and the screenwriter's agreement, and in other ways is unique to the theater. The playwright, like the book author, often conceives and writes the play independently, rarely writing for hire as the screenwriter usually does. Also, like the book author, the playwright generally retains a good deal of control over what happens to the play; indeed, the playwright generally shares approval over the selection of the director, cast, designers, and other creative personnel associated with a production, so much so that she probably has more to do with the ultimate outcome of her work than the book author.

Conversely, the fact that the playwright (of a Broadway production) has a permanent organization, the Dramatists Guild, to represent her interests vis-à-vis those who acquire rights to her work is more reminiscent of the screenwriter's situation, although the Dramatists Guild's influence is rather less pervasive than the WGA's, primarily because the Dramatists Guild is not a union and does not wield the power of a labor union. Ultimately, however, the theater has unique customs and practices that are reflected in the typical playwright's agreement.

When is the typical playwright agreement made?

Often a producer has an idea for a play and hires people to write it. This occurs most frequently with musicals where the producer assembles in advance the necessary creative contributors, including book writer, composer, and lyricist. And sometimes, the creative folks will approach a producer with their idea for a show. Even in these situations, however, the producer will rarely own the finished product, as the producer of a film does. Rather, the writers of the play will usually own the finished product, subject to the specific production rights granted to the original producer.

But in many instances the negotiations for the typical playwright's agreement begin only after the playwright has written the play, or at least a draft of the play that may be revised during production. The dramatist's agreement, called a production agreement, generally gives the producer (one or more individuals or companies) the right to produce the play in a particular venue (i.e., a city, state, country, or territory) or in a particular theater or size of theater, provided that the producer presents the first performance of the play before a paying audience by an outside date specified in the contract.

For example, a typical off-Broadway production contract would provide that the producer must present the first paid public performance in an off-Broadway theater in New York City within a stated period (perhaps 6 months or a year) from the date of the agreement. "Off-Broadway theater" must be defined, and the location of the theater is not necessarily determinative. According to commonly used definitions, the size of the house controls that determination. The producer may also have the right to extend the outside date of the first performance by the payment of additional sums to the author.

What does the producer get?

The producer's right to produce the play is an "option." Staying with the above example, during the producer's option period the producer will try to raise the necessary funds to produce the play, usually from private sources. The customary investment structure is the "limited partnership" or "limited liability company," where investors purchase limited interests in the entity that will produce the play and the producer acts as general partner or managing member. At the same time, the producer will try to assemble the best team for the project—the general manager (responsible for the day-to-day management of the production) and the creative team: director, designers, and perhaps key cast members who will best bring to life the playwright's vision.

The option is exercised by the producer's presentation of the play in accordance with the contract with the playwright—that is, within the time and at the type of theater specified in the agreement. When that happens, the producer has the right to continue to present the play indefinitely until the production closes. In addition, if the necessary number of performances are presented, the producer also becomes entitled to acquire additional production rights in the play; for example, the right to present the play in other countries, on tour, or in other ways and to share in subsidiary rights as discussed below.

What payments are made to the playwright for the producer's option?

When an option contract is made (or extended), a payment is usually made to the playwright—by screenwriter (or even publishing) standards, rather modest. One possible reason playwrights have more control over their plays is that they generally share more of the risk. The playwright's hope of realizing real money from the play depends on its presentation. Also, although the sums paid on execution or extension of the option are nonrefundable, they are often treated as an advance against the royalties the playwright may earn in whole or in part in the future.

What kinds of productions are there?

There are several kinds of productions a playwright may authorize, including nonprofit and commercial productions. Frequently, particularly in the early life of a play, it may first be produced at one of the many regional theaters throughout the country or at a "subscription" theater in New York. These theaters, usually operated on a nonprofit basis, present initial limited-run productions. This gives the playwright an opportunity to revise the play in a production setting prior to its presentation on a more commercial basis.

The agreement with the regional or subscription theater sometimes includes an option to produce a subsequent commercial production, unless a commercial producer already holds the rights. If a regional or subscription production is particularly successful, that production may be moved to a commercial theater and reorganized as a commercial production by the regional or subscription producer, alone or with others. For example, *A Chorus Line*, one of the longest-running musicals on Broadway, began as a limited engagement at the New York Shakespeare Festival, and *Steel Magnolias* began at WPA in New York before moving off-Broadway and then to the screen.

If the regional or subscription theater does not wish to move its production immediately to a commercial setting, it may still have the right to produce a commercial production of that play for a certain period following the close of its limited run. It may produce a subsequent commercial production itself or more likely assign its option to an independent commercial producer in exchange for a flat fee or a royalty. An off-Broadway production is a commercial production, as is a "first-class" production, which includes any production presented in a Broadway theater. A commercial production is one that has the potential of an unlimited run (as opposed to the limited engagement of a nonprofit production) and gets its production funding from investors seeking a profit. The standard terms of the playwright's contract—indeed, in some instances what is required by the Dramatists Guild—depend on the kinds of productions included in the producer's option.

What options are covered by the Dramatists Guild contract?

The Dramatists Guild has promulgated form contracts for virtually every type of production—first-class, off-Broadway, regional. However, it does not follow that these agreements are actually used. For example, although the Guild's Approved Production Contract (APC) is often used for Broadway and other first-class productions, the Guild's off-Broadway agreement is almost never used. This is because the Approved Production Contract was intensely negotiated between the League of New York Theaters and Producers and the Dramatists Guild before it was issued, while negotiations between off-Broadway producers and the Guild over the off-Broadway contract broke down, and the Guild decided to promulgate its own agreement anyway, hoping it would be used. But it almost never is. As one observer noted, "It has never been accepted as a viable contract by knowledgeable attorneys and agents working in theater, although some agents representing authors of plays have tried to impose it on producers. . . . The contract is so 'pro-Author' that it would be difficult to find financing for any play acquired by a producer pursuant to its terms."

Once the option agreement is signed, what happens next?

If the option is for a commercial production, the producer has to raise the necessary production funds. If it's for a nonprofit regional or subscription production, the producer will already have the funding and will proceed directly to production.

Once production funding is secured, the rehearsal period can begin. The playwright always has the right to attend rehearsals. Usually the playwright has the right to approve the director, designers, and perhaps most important, the cast. The playwright will also generally promise to work with the director and producer in rewriting that may be necessary from a production standpoint, although the playwright has the last word on whether changes to the play are acceptable. If rehearsals are away from the playwright's city of residence, the agreement will generally require the producer to provide the playwright round-trip transportation and a per diem for expenses. Whether the transportation is to be first class and the amount of the per diem are often hotly negotiated.

Assuming all goes reasonably well, the play will first be presented to the public in "preview performances" where the producer and director can assess the production with live audiences. Additional rewrites and revisions may be necessary, and the industry routinely buzzes with gossip about changes being made at this point. After the previews, there is generally an official "opening" to which critics are invited. The playwright has the right, by contract, to purchase a given number of "house seats" (seats in the front center section of the house) for each performance and in most cases a few more for the opening. Once the play opens, everyone involved hopes it runs for a long time, because if it doesn't, no one—the producer, the director, the playwright, and certainly not the investors—will make much money from it.

How does the playwright make money?

With a regional or subscription production, the playwright shouldn't expect to make much money. Such productions don't pay well and generally are not presented in large theaters. Since payment is most often based on the gross, and since the gross is directly related to the size of the house, a small house means a small gross, which means little money for the author. But the key reason there isn't much money here is that the productions are generally for limited runs, so there isn't an opportunity for extended ticket sales.

It's only when a run is potentially unlimited that there are real possibilities for financial gain for a playwright. How that gain is computed requires some explanation since nearly every agreement contains one traditional method of payment and an alternate method, which today is almost always used.

The custom in the theater for decades was that the playwright's compensation was a royalty computed as a percentage of the "gross weekly box-office receipts"; thus, by definition, the more weeks the play runs, the more gross there will be for the author's royalties. And unlike the screenwriter's net profits, the definition of "gross" is short and uniformly accepted: all income from the sale of tickets, less commissions for theater parties, discount and cut-rate sales, admission taxes, charge-card expenses, amounts equal to New York City's former amusement tax (which are now sent to union pension and welfare funds), subscription fees, Actors' Fund benefits, and so-called "theater renovation fees." Often, the royalty percentage increases when the production has recouped all of its production costs (i.e., the production has generated sufficient income to "reimburse" the producer for the costs of producing and keeping the play running).

In straight (i.e., nonmusical) plays, the playwright's royalty for a first-class production under the Dramatists Guild APC is 5 percent of the gross, which increases to 10 percent on recoupment of production costs. For an off-Broadway or second-class production, the pre-recoupment royalty is generally 5 percent or 6 percent, which may increase to 6 percent or 7 percent after recoupment. For musicals, the off-Broadway or second-class royalty is almost always 6 percent and increases after recoupment are less frequent. For a Broadway or first-class musical production, the authors are paid 4.5 percent increasing to 6 percent after 110 percent recoupment. This percentage is shared by the book writer, composer, and lyricist as they may agree in their collaboration agreement (the most common agreement is for equal shares). Of course, musicals generally are in larger theaters, so even 1.5 percent of the gross can represent a good deal of money on a weekly basis, especially when the price for a ticket to a Broadway musical can now exceed $150.

Typically, not only the authors but also the director, producer, theater owner, and perhaps even the designers and stars will be entitled to a percentage of the gross. Under such a "financial food chain," the royalty participants eat first; the fixed costs of running the production are then taken from what's left of the gross; any advertising and promotional costs follow; a reserve for emergencies is set aside; and finally the investors share what little of the gross may be left. As a result, even with seemingly successful productions, investors do not receive profit participations very quickly or (comparatively speaking) in especially large amounts.

Because investment in a commercial theatrical production is at best an extremely speculative venture, investors understandably do not want to be at the end of the "food chain." To attract investors, producers have created a way for everyone to participate in whatever funds come in: the "royalty pool," the alternative method of payment mentioned above. Nearly all playwright agreements now provide for a pool from which a production's weekly fixed costs are paid first. Whatever is left ("operating profits") is distributed to investors and royalty recipients, from 30 percent to as high as 50 percent being allocated to the royalty recipients. Thus, if all of the royalty participants (e.g., authors, producer, director, theater owner, etc.) are collectively entitled to 12 percent of the gross and the playwright to 6 percent under the pool approach, the playwright would get half of the operating profits allocated to royalty participants, reflecting the playwright's share of the total royalty participation. To ensure that the playwright's payments do not fall below a specified level, royalty-pool provisions guarantee that a minimum payment per royalty point will be made weekly. That minimum can be as low as $150 for off-Broadway or second-class productions, and as high (for some well-established playwrights) as $1,000 per point in first-class or Broadway productions.

What does the producer get for producing the play?

It depends on the kind of producer. A commercial producer generally receives a share of the gross as a "producer's royalty" and will continue to participate in gross distributions, or in the pool if one is in effect. Most producers also take a weekly cash "office charge" and many take a weekly cash "executive producer" fee. If the production runs long enough to recoup production costs and repay investors, the limited partnership or LLC formed to produce the play will typically be earning partnership profits, and these profits are shared by the investors and the producer. In addition, if enough performances are presented, the producer may also earn the right to present the play elsewhere (with the same income opportunities available)—on tour, in foreign countries, and, perhaps most important, to participate in subsidiary rights income.

The subsidiary rights ("sub rights") of a play refer to its future exploitation, including other productions of the play—for example, in foreign languages or stock or amateur versions (which rights can be quite lucrative with plays that had successful commercial runs)—and the right to base a motion picture or television production on the play, although those rights are frequently withheld by the underlying rights owners.

The justification for a producer's participation in sub-rights income is that by presenting the play and introducing it to the public, the producer has contributed to the value of the play and should therefore participate in the fruits of its future exploitation. There can be no question that the longer a play runs, the more attention the public has paid to it; that recognition alone can be said to increase its value. Accordingly, at least in theory, the longer a play runs, the greater the producer's participation in sub rights should be. For example, a typical off-Broadway agreement might give the producer the following percentages of the playwright's income from subsidiary-rights deals made within a given period (say 10 years) after the close of the producer's run of the play: 10 percent if the play runs for at least 21 consecutive paid performances; 20 percent if the play runs for at least 42 consecutive paid performances; 30 percent if the play runs for at least 56 paid performances; 40 percent if the play runs for 65 consecutive paid performances or more. For the purposes of computing the number of performances, provided the play officially opens in New York City, the first paid performance shall be deemed to be the first performance, however only eight paid previews will be counted in this computation.

A commercial producer of a second-class production rarely receives more than 40 percent of the playwright's sub-rights income, but the producer of a first-class or Broadway production under the APC may receive up to 50 percent of certain types of sub-rights income.

What does a nonprofit regional or subscription producer get?

A regional or subscription-theater producer generally gets, at most, whatever may be left of ticket income after everyone else involved with the production is paid. And since most such producers can rarely pay their production costs from ticket-sale income and rely heavily on charitable contributions, they generally don't get anything from their productions.

However, if the play is produced in a subsequent production within a given period after the close of its production, the playwright's agreement with the regional-subscription producer usually provides for a royalty percentage of 1 percent or 2 percent of gross or a pro rata share of the royalty pool, whichever is applicable. The agreement might also require the playwright to secure for that producer a share in the net profits of a subsequent commercial company's rendition of the play. Also, the agreement often provides for that producer to receive a percentage of sub-rights income—especially if no gross or net profit share becomes available—since these theaters present new and untested works that continue to be developed during the production and are thus entitled to share in some of the play's future success. Rarely, however, will this percentage be as high as 10 percent, and it is often as low as 5 percent, although such sub-rights participations are in addition to the royalty or pool participation mentioned above. As a result, when a play meets with commercial success, the playwright is only one of the beneficiaries.

What happens when a producer commissions a play?

A producer may have an idea for a play and, like a film producer, seek the right person (or persons if it's a musical, as commissioned plays often are) to write it. Often, the producer bases his idea for a play on a work in another medium, such as a book or movie. For example, one of the producers of the hit musical *La Cage aux Folles* first secured the stage rights to the property, originally presented in the form of nonmusical movie and stage play, and then assembled the team that wrote the book, music, and lyrics for the musical. An agreement like this usually provides that the writers must contribute material satisfactory to the producer, but the producer generally does not have the sweeping rights of a film producer to do pretty much whatever she wants with the material submitted. The agreement may also provide that the producer has the right to replace the writers, subject to payment for material used. The producer may also have a limited continuing participation (similar to a nonprofit theater's participation, as described above) in future productions and subsidiary rights.

THE RIGHTS-ACQUISITION AGREEMENT

All of the contracts discussed so far involve the initial exploitation of an author's work. But what happens when someone wants to create a work in one medium, say a movie or a play, that is based on something written for another medium, such as a novel, a biography, or even a song? The contract is called a rights-acquisition agreement. From the author's point of view—assuming the author owns the underlying rights—such agreements can be depressing and burdensome. They are usually lengthy, involve assigning away most of the author's rights in the work, and in the short term do not involve much money. In the long term, however, a rights-acquisition agreement can be extremely lucrative for the author, and in some cases can offer a new world of opportunity for the fortunate writer willing and able to make the transition to writing for another medium.

Almost always, the original author will have to give up control over the fate of his work. As a well-known literary agent specializing in rights acquisition agreements has put it, "If the most important thing to the writer is that the film be faithful to the book, don't sell the rights; if that's not so important, sell the rights for as much as you can, and don't see the movie!"

What does the purchaser acquire?

Virtually all the available rights in the work—and some that don't yet exist! In the first place, the "property" (the play or book or whatever) is invariably defined very broadly; it may include all "plots, themes, narrative, dialogue, titles, characters and copyright thereof." So even though the purchaser is ostensibly acquiring only rights to this one work, by so defining the property, the exclusive grant of rights to this purchaser may prevent the author from selling movie rights to another work that involves the same character or theme.

Entire paragraphs (indeed pages) of the contract are often devoted to describing in exquisite detail the rights being granted by the author to the purchaser. A motion picture rights-acquisition agreement usually includes all exclusive rights in the property, including the right to create films and taped productions based on the property, in any language, with music synchronized or otherwise; to record such films and productions, using any processes now known or hereafter invented; to exhibit, distribute, and otherwise exploit the created productions in any manner whatsoever, including but not limited to theatrically, nontheatrically, on free or pay television, broadcast or cable, in home video, and so on; to produce and present remakes and sequels; to exploit certain limited publication rights; to release a soundtrack; to exploit merchandising rights (e.g., bed linens, clothing, lunch boxes, ad infinitum) and commercial rights (using the property to sell toothpaste, for example).

If the purchaser is acquiring theatrical dramatization or musicalization rights (as the creators of *Cabaret* did in acquiring Christopher Isherwood's "I Am a Camera"), the agreement usually includes all the rights mentioned above and others. But these days, plays will regularly be produced commercially even if movie rights in the play are not acquired.

In any case, the acquisition agreement invariably includes the right to make changes of any kind to the property. The author specifically waives any right of *droit moral* (discussed in Chapter 2). The purchaser can change any character, add to or delete from the story, and even combine the property with a completely different property. In most instances, the author will have no rights of approval unless he has tremendous bargaining power. Even in those rare cases, however, the author's rights of approval are usually quite limited.

What does the author keep?

Book publication rights (in the case of a published work acquired for adaptation to another medium) and in other instances the right to continue to exploit the work in its original medium. Motion picture and television rights acquisition agreements sometimes do not include live dramatic or musical rights, which are often reserved to the granting party along with the right to release a cast album. However, the fact that an author may still grant a third party the right to create a dramatic production based on the property does not necessarily mean that a film could be based on that play, because of the breadth of the original acquisition.

Book authors generally retain certain rights to write sequels for publication ("author-written sequels"), although this would not diminish the rights the producer acquires in the characters. As a result, an author can write a written sequel using a particular character while the producer can produce a filmed sequel using the same character, and they can be entirely different stories.

Usually, however, the author will not be able to exploit any of these reserved rights immediately, except for the right to continue to exploit the property in its original format. There is generally a stated period during which the author is required to "hold back" from exercising or permitting others to exercise those rights. The hold-back period is often five years from the release of the first motion picture based on the work or seven years from the date of the agreement, whichever occurs first. The author's rights for an author-written sequel may be even more restricted since the purchaser often insists on a right of "first negotiation" (the author has to negotiate with the purchaser before approaching a third party), "last refusal" (the purchaser has the right to meet the terms a third party has offered for the rights), or even an option to acquire the movie or television rights to the author-written sequel.

How is a typical acquisition agreement set up?

On rare occasions a purchaser will acquire all the rights outright and will pay the full purchase price immediately. But far more often the purchaser wants to make sure that she can acquire the rights and that she really wants to. The preliminary work can be extensive; for motion pictures, for example, it can include actually causing a screenplay to be written. What is usually most critical to a potential purchaser deciding whether to acquire the rights is whether he can obtain a commitment for funding or the actual funding necessary to see the project through.

The acquisition contract is premised on this two-stage process and results in two separate but interconnected legal agreements whereby the purchaser acquires an option (the first agreement) to activate the actual rights acquisition (the second agreement). In the option agreement, the purchaser pays the author for the right for a limited period to acquire the property under the terms and conditions set forth in the rights-acquisition agreement, which is prepared and attached to the option agreement. The option agreement often provides that the option period can be extended one, two, or even three times beyond the original period, provided timely notice and additional payments are given to the author.

A typical option in a movie or television rights-acquisition agreement will provide for an initial period of one year, renewable for one or two additional years. When the purchaser is acquiring the right to create a theatrical play based on the property, he will want even more time since he must first have the play written and then get the production financed and then find a theater (a difficult task on Broadway where theaters are limited and in great demand). The option period is almost always extendable for reasons of *force majeure* (i.e., acts of God, war, catastrophe, and perhaps most significantly, strikes, although there is often a requirement that to extend the option term, the *force majeure* must directly and materially affect the agreement). Such clauses offered significant consolation to the various producers affected by the 1988 WGA writers' strike since they meant that as long as the writers couldn't write, the option clock was not ticking.

The acquisition agreement provides for payments to the author for the purchase of the property. The purchaser can exercise the option at any time by sending the author written notice together with that part of the purchase price due on exercise. However, many agreements also provide that the option is deemed exercised by taking certain actions, with payment then due for that exercise. For a movie or television production, the acquisition agreement often provides that the commencement of principal photography constitutes the exercise of the option. In the theater, an option is deemed exercised by the production of a play before a paying audience in the type of theater contemplated by the agreement.

What kind of money are we talking about?

Prices for an option can vary widely, from a nominal payment (say, $1,000) to six figures or more, depending on a variety of factors, including how hungry the market is for the property, the form the property is in, its popularity, when (and if) it's been published, the author's track record, and how sure the purchaser is of being able to proceed with it. The first option payment is almost always applicable (treated as an advance) against the ultimate purchase price. Payments made for extensions of the option term are usually not (or only partially) applied against the purchase price. A rule of thumb is that the price of an option represents 10 percent of the purchase price.

Like the option price, the ultimate purchase price can vary widely, depending upon many of the factors listed above as well as the work's age, scope, story, name recognition, potential cast, and the number of other offers at hand. The parties may include "escalators" in the purchase price to reward a property that does well in its initial medium; for example, the acquisition price for a novel may increase depending on the number of weeks it appears on the best-seller list or the sale of book-club rights. The purchase price may be made adjustable during the production of the film, so that the price could be set as a percentage of the final approved production budget but not less than a stated minimum or more than a stated maximum. In television, the purchase price may be one figure for a two-hour movie, with increases for any film longer than that.

As with the bonus, deferred, and contingent forms of compensation paid to screenwriters, there are additional forms of compensation customarily paid to the rights owner. For example, as in the screenwriter's contract, the author-owner will often be entitled to contingent compensation in the form of a participation in net profits of from 2.5 to 5 percent, but such participations will be subject to the same limitations presented by the definition of net profits discussed above. If the first production is intended for initial release on television and the film is subsequently released theatrically in the United States or abroad, additional payments to the owner are customary, usually half the purchase price on domestic release and half on foreign release. The owner often receives additional compensation if a television series is based on the owner's work.

If the acquisition agreement is for theatrical dramatization rights, in addition to the purchase price (which will usually be modest when compared to the price for film rights) the agreement will provide for a royalty equal to one-third of the royalties paid to the composer, lyricist, and book writer jointly for musicals and 30 percent to 50 percent of the total paid to the playwright and the underlying rights owner jointly for a straight play, which royalties to be based on the play's gross receipts, with a possible increase after the producer has recouped production costs, subject to participation in a royalty pool. Finally, if there is a sale of subsidiary rights in a play based on the property that is the subject of the acquisition agreement, the owner will usually participate in the playwright's share of subsidiary rights income in the same proportion that the rights seller's royalty from a theatrical production bears to the total royalty of the rights holder combined with that of all parties who wrote the play.

For example, the musical *Les Misérables* was based on Victor Hugo's novel of the same name. Since Hugo (1802–1885) was long dead, that property was in the public domain, and no rights payment was necessary. Suppose, however, that it was still protected and that the theatrical producers of the play had to pay Hugo a royalty from theatrical productions, which they agreed would be 2 percent of the gross (one-third of the amount jointly due the composer, lyricist and book writer, assuming that they collectively received 6 percent of the gross). Finally, suppose the film rights in the play were sold to a film producer for $100,000. After deducting a 40 percent share for the theater producer, Hugo would be entitled to $15,000, his 2 percent royalty being one-third of 6 percent, which is the total royalty of all of the authors plus the rights holder, so he's entitled to 25 percent of the film subsidiary rights payment. However, if the play's authors also wrote the screenplay for the film version and received additional compensation (over and above the rights payment) for those services, Hugo would not be entitled to any participation in that payment.

Does the original author receive credit in a subsequent production?

Yes, although in the theater the credit is often smaller than (usually half) the size of the credit given to the authors of the new material. The credit to the original author will generally appear wherever and whenever those authors' names appear. In film and television, the credit to the original author generally appears on a "single card" (no other credits appear at the same time) and in paid advertising in which any other writer is credited. Unlike the theater, in film and television the original author's credit is the same size as that of the screenwriter.

What other rights might the original author obtain?

Some fortunate authors are able secure the opportunity to write at least the first draft of the adapted work. This can provide not only additional income to the author (above the rights-acquisition price) but also exposure and experience in writing in a different medium. Unfortunately, it is relatively rare for the original author to get this opportunity.

If the purchaser does nothing with the rights, can the owner get them back?

Until recently, the answer was often yes for motion pictures and always yes for the theater. If a movie production based on the property was not begun within a stated period from the date of the agreement (say, seven years), the acquisition agreement provided that the rights would revert to the owner, although sometimes the owner had to repay the producer what she had received from the producer and sometimes the owner also had to repay the producer for costs incurred in connection with the development of the property (e.g., payments made to screenwriters, etc., to develop the property). Since the owner would usually exercise this right only if another producer was interested in acquiring the rights, such payments would normally be made by that second producer.

These days, however, movie producers increasingly insist that the rights to a property cannot revert under any circumstances. Although producers argue that the cost of a rights acquisition justifies their continued ownership of the rights whether or not they do anything with them, that view seems unpersuasive in light of the importance to the author's career of a film based on his book (not simply having sold the movie rights). The producers' argument also seems to ignore the tremendous income potential that a production has for the author. For these reasons, many authors and their agents are insisting on a right of reversion, even if it means losing a rights sale.

CONTRACTS INVOLVING PHOTOGRAPHERS

There are two principal ways photographers can make a living as such: as salaried employees of an entity (a newspaper or magazine, advertising agency, government body, or business corporation) or as freelance self-employed professionals hired by others for assignments. In almost every relevant way, the contracts and legal rights applicable to the employee-photographer are different from those applicable to the freelancer. For the most part, this section will discuss the customary contracts made by freelance photographers.

What rights do employee-photographers have vis-à-vis their employers?

Only those rights set forth in their employment contracts. The law, including in particular the U.S. Copyright Act, assumes that all legal rights, including all copyrights, in the photographs they take for their employers belong automatically and for all purposes to the employer. The applicable legal doctrine is "work made for hire," which simply means that the work product of the photographer is created by her as a functionary of the employer and for its benefit, and the employer as a legal matter is considered the creator of the work and the owner of all legal rights in it.

As a result, unless the parties agree otherwise, the employee has no individual right to use or exploit work created for his employer, and the employee could violate the legal rights of (and jeopardize his or her employment with) the employer by attempting to do so. Of course, the employer might permit the employee to make certain uses of, and perhaps even sell, such work, but such permission would have to be specifically sought and obtained. On the other hand, unlike their freelance counterparts, employee-photographers do not have any separate overhead expenses (for studios, cameras, lighting, etc.) and can count on a regular paycheck (and other benefits).

Significantly, in recent years some employers have been open to "co-ownership" relationships with their employee-photographers, in which the photographer may have certain specified rights in her work. In appropriate circumstances, such photographers should seek such relationships with the right to separately exploit their work, without damaging or conflicting with the rights of their employers.

What kinds of assignments do freelance photographers receive?

There is probably no limit to the kinds of assignments freelance photographers receive, and the specific aspects of those assignments (including the method of payment, working conditions, and rights to the work) can vary as widely as the assignments themselves. For example, there are enormous differences between an assignment from the local newspaper to cover a press conference at City Hall and an assignment from a major corporation to take the photographs for its annual report; an assignment to photograph a wedding and an assignment to take photographs for a national advertising campaign for an exotic perfume (or fast food chain); an assignment to take publicity photographs for an entertainer and an assignment to shoot an elaborate layout for a fashion magazine. These kinds of assignments require different talents and temperaments. They also inevitably involve different kinds of contracts and legal relationships.

Although there are any number of assignments a freelance photographer might receive, all probably fall into one of two major categories: "editorial" (photographs designed for use in the editorial as distinct from advertising or promotional parts of a newspaper, magazine, or book), and "commercial" (all other assignments, including advertising, corporate, promotional, and other internal business uses, such as resources for lawyers, doctors, designers, builders, etc.). Where appropriate, the differences between editorial and commercial assignments will be discussed on the following pages.

What is the significance of who owns the copyright in the photographs?

The owner of the copyright in a photograph, as with any other created work, is the person who controls how that work can be used and exploited, not just in the immediate present but also in the future. In the case of "work made for hire," that person is the employer, and the employee-photographer has no say in that control. In contrast, with freelance assignments it is the photographer and not the employer who is the owner of the copyright, at least until the parties agree otherwise. Thus, subject to the contract with the party who assigns work to the photographer (the "client"), the photographer controls and can exploit all uses of the work not specifically granted ("licensed") to the client. The ownership of the copyright in the work can be of enormous importance to the freelance photographer.

How do contracts deal with the ownership of copyrights in the assigned work?

Although under the law the freelance photographer is presumed to be the owner of all her photographs, it is not uncommon in both editorial and commercial assignments for the client to claim and/or seek to acquire all those copyright rights from the freelance photographer.

Essentially, those clients seek to accomplish this in two ways. First, those contracts (in both editorial and commercial assignments) may provide that the work shall be considered "work made for hire" and thus the copyright property of the client and not the photographer. Under current law, if the work fits within one of the categories where such contracts are permitted (including in newspapers or magazines) and the work is "specially ordered and commissioned" for that use, such contracts will generally be upheld.

Most freelance photographers who find such "work-for-hire" provisions in contracts try to have those provisions deleted so that they can retain at least some rights to their work, but often— probably almost inevitably with many clients—the clients insist that those provisions remain in the agreement. Even where such provisions remain, however, it may be possible for the photographer to be permitted some limited rights to use and exploit the work, such as use in the photographer's promotional materials and display in any show of the photographer's work. And photographers who are asked to sign such "work-for-hire" contracts can try to negotiate additional compensation because all rights in the work are being granted to the client.

Second, the photographer is asked to transfer (in effect, sell) his copyrights in the work to the client in the contract confirming the assignment. Here too, most freelance photographers confronted with such provisions will try to resist them or at least obtain greater compensation and some limited rights in those contracts. In some cases, an employer may be willing to accept an "unlimited" license to use the work instead of a transfer of the entire copyright.

In practice, most clients (including publications, advertising agencies, corporations, etc.) will have well-established policies, and experienced photographers will know what to expect when offered assignments from them. If a photographer does not know a client's policies and wants to know as soon as possible, she should raise the issue immediately upon being offered the assignment to avoid confusion and misunderstanding later. And photographers can always refuse any assignments that contain provisions they consider unfair or inappropriate.

The most difficult situations arise when the photographer does not know that the client expects to own the copyrights in the work until the assignment has been completed and the photographer requests payment. Such situations can create serious tension between the parties and lead to litigation. However, such situations are increasingly rare, partly because reputable clients disclose in advance their copyright expectations and partly because photographers have learned that they should be clear about those expectations before they accept the assignment.

It is far more common in commercial photography than in editorial photography for the client to expect the photographer to transfer copyrights in the work to the client. In fact, in most editorial assignments for newspapers and magazines, where the need for the work is immediate and short-lived, the client usually expects only "one-time use" in the work and is willing to let the photographer own and control all other rights in it. Such clients will generally pay less for those assignments than if greater rights are transferred to them. Also, some magazines, particularly those for whom photographs represent an important part of their publications and who tend to use them more than once, expect to acquire the copyrights (sometimes referred to as "all-rights" assignments) and are prepared to pay for those greater rights.

What else do most photography contracts include?

Unlike the contracts that are commonly used to reflect book publishing, screenwriting, and theater agreements, which often can run for dozens of excruciating pages, the contracts generally used for freelance photography assignments are often little more than one or two pages. Most clients, especially those who make such assignments on a regular basis, develop their own relatively simple forms, often called work or purchase orders. Those forms generally identify the assignment, the completion or delivery date, the compensation (or method of computing it), the photographer's expenses, the copyright ownership (including any rights the photographer will have), and various representations, warranties, and indemnities running from the photographer to the client. Such contracts may also require the photographer to deliver to the client signed releases from any people (and occasionally for places and things) appearing in the photographs. Some of these issues are discussed more fully below.

Many photographers also develop their own form contracts, often denominated confirmations or invoices, which they submit to their clients. Those contracts often contain provisions that flatly contradict provisions in the client's form contract, such as providing that the photographer owns the copyright in the work and narrowly limiting the rights being acquired by the client, and both sides may think that their contracts govern the assignment. In the end, however, it is the client who will probably have the last word if the photographer wants to get paid for the assignment and receive future assignments from that client.

It is possible—although increasingly rare—that the parties' agreement will not be in writing but will be an oral agreement or entirely (or almost entirely) unspoken. (These days, oral assignments will usually be followed by paperwork and/or the client insists on a "blanket" agreement to cover all assignments.) But sometimes an editor of a newspaper or magazine might simply telephone a freelance photographer and ask her to cover an event without saying more about the assignment. In such circumstances, the contract of the parties will be deemed consistent with their prior relationship or be inferred from the established customs and practices that generally apply to such assignments. Importantly, neither a "work-for-hire" relationship nor a transfer of copyright can be accomplished in such an oral or unspoken contract since the law requires a written agreement for those purposes.

One further point should be made. Sometimes it may not be clear exactly who the client is, especially where an advertising agency is hiring the photographer to take photographs for a client of the agency. Who is responsible to the photographer for payment and for honoring the other terms of the contract? If there is any doubt on this issue, the photographer should attempt to make clear in the contract who the real client is.

How are freelance photographers paid?

In a variety of ways, depending on the nature of the assignment and the policies and practices of both parties. Many assignments provide that the photographer will be paid at an hourly, daily, or weekly rate, regardless of the number of photographs taken or ultimately used. In fact, these days the almost universal practice is for clients to offer a specified day rate for the right to use all the output of the photographer on the assignment, with an additional payment if the photographer's work appears on the cover. (Not surprisingly, these days the client will also expect, for no additional payment, the right to use that output in social media and otherwise on the Internet.) In most cases, regardless of the form of compensation, the client will also reimburse the photographer for at least some of his expenses on the assignment, although those expenses may have to be approved in advance. Also, particularly where the photographer has doubts about the reliability (or solvency) of the client, it would be prudent to add to the contract the time of payment and a provision that the client will not be authorized to use the work until full payment has been made.

The photographer should always feel free to (try to) negotiate the best compensation for the assignment, and it can happen, especially if the client wants the special talents (or availability) of the photographer, that the photographer will be able to negotiate terms more favorable than originally offered.

As a general proposition, commercial photography pays better than editorial, at least in monetary compensation. However, editorial photography, especially when it appears in the most "sophisticated" publications, can provide greater exposure and prestige, and, if the photographer retains rights in the work after the assignment, the potential for future exploitation of the work. Contracts for editorial assignments usually provide that if the client makes use of the work beyond the one-time use originally contemplated, additional payments will be made.

What kinds of representations, warranties, and indemnities do photography contracts require?

Photography agreements are similar to the agreements book authors, screenwriters, and playwrights are often asked to sign. They usually provide that the photographer "represents" and "warrants" to the client that the work does not violate any copyrights or other property rights of third parties, does not contain anything that is libelous, invade anyone's right of privacy or publicity, or otherwise present any legal risk to the client. Such provisions also usually provide that the photographer will indemnify and hold the client harmless from any expenses or damages incurred as a result of any breach or alleged breach of any of those representations or warranties. In many respects (including in particular the obligation to indemnify for an "alleged breach," where the photographer may not have done anything wrong), such provisions seem especially harsh and unfair. However, as in the other media where similar requirements are common, it will often be difficult to persuade the client to delete or modify these provisions, but this does not mean the effort should not be made.

Especially when the client requests the photographer to make such representations, the photographer should at least consider requesting corresponding representations from the client. Through such provisions, the client would "cover" the photographer if claims are made against the photographer based on the use of the work by the client, anything added to or removed from the work by the client, or anything else done by the client over which the photographer had no control.

What about credit to the photographer?

An important component of the contract for freelance photography is the credit to be given the photographer when the work is used by the client. If the contract does not deal with credit, it is likely the client will have no obligation to credit the photographer. The photographer should insist that the work be credited to her, along with (if appropriate) a copyright notice in the name of the photographer, although many clients will resist these kinds of specific obligations. This is particularly important if the photographer expects a particular form of byline and copyright notice in a book. Under the Copyright Act, the omission of a separate copyright notice in the photographer's name will normally not jeopardize that copyright since the copyright notice covering the work as a whole will be deemed to protect the separately owned components of the work.

When is it necessary to obtain releases from the subjects of photographs?

Whenever the contract says you must. Beyond that, the answer depends on a variety of factors, including the circumstances of the shooting and the intended use of the photographs. Photographs of public events or everyday street scenes that are used for editorial purposes normally do not require any permission or release from the subjects, at least where there is a "reasonable" editorial basis for their use.

In a famous case, a magazine used a photograph of a large family to illustrate an article about how injections of caffeine supposedly increased the fertility of a man's sperm. The family did not consent; indeed, was not even aware that the photograph was to be used in this way, and did not use caffeine or any other fertility enhancements. New York's highest court rejected the family's claim of invasion of privacy, finding that the photograph had a "reasonable relationship" to the article and that the magazine therefore had the legal right to use it in that way.

Similarly, in an earlier case, the *New York Times Magazine* published an article on the "black middle class" and used a photograph of a well-dressed black man on a New York street to illustrate the article. That man did not consent to that use, wasn't aware of it until it was published, and did not agree with the thesis of the article. But the same New York court rejected his privacy suit, holding that as long as the photograph was reasonably related to the article, it was immune from legal liability. (While the court absolved the magazine of liability for that reason, it also held that the photographer could be sued for selling the photograph to the magazine. However, the New York legislature soon thereafter amended the New York "Right of Privacy" statute to make it clear that where the publication can't be sued for any such use, neither can the photographer.)

But photographs of people that are to be used in advertisements or for other commercial purposes, even if taken at public events or street scenes, generally do require written releases or permission from those people. This is because the law in most states protects individuals (whether or not they're well known or have any publicity value) from the commercial (as distinct from editorial) use of their likenesses.

In some cases, even photographs destined for editorial use may require releases. This is especially true where the shooting involves professional models, celebrities, or others who have been asked and agree to be photographed by the photographer. In such cases, the relationship between the photographer and the subject can be seen as a contractual one, and it's always possible that the terms of that "contract" will be disputed later. For example, the subject of the photos might claim that she was promised approval rights over the photos to be used or that they could be used only one time in one specified publication or that the ownership rights in them would belong to the subject. To avoid future confrontations, it is desirable to get a release or other contract from the subject confirming the terms applicable to the shooting.

What happens when a photographer wants to exploit rights to preexisting work?

In addition to work created pursuant to an assignment, most photographers create work on their own, for pleasure, for future exploitation, or both. Also, photographers who do not convey to the client all rights to work created on an assignment will own and control rights to the non-conveyed work. As a result, most freelance photographers own rights to a large stock of their photographs.

There are two principal ways photographers can exploit that work. First, they can attempt to exploit those rights themselves by letting potential users (e.g., newspapers, magazines, advertising agencies) know of the availability of the work and by entering into agreements for the use of such work. Probably the most common way photographers do this these days is to display their works on their own and their agents' websites and social media pages and through such online hosting services as PhotoShelter, where a photographer can set up galleries of his work that can be password protected. (Less digitally, photographers can prepare and send promotional material describing the work and its availability, running appropriate advertisements in trade publications and the like, and visiting potential users face-to-face.)

In most cases, the license fees payable for limited ("one-time") use of preexisting work are fairly modest, ranging from as little as $25 to several hundred and (infrequently) many thousands of dollars. Photographers will obviously have to devote considerable time and energy exploiting their preexisting work if they expect to realize significant income in this way.

Which leads to the other way photographers can exploit that work—entering into agreements with online photo agencies like Getty Images and Shutterstock, which have massive and intricate web-based sites that allow online searches for and—for specified payments—the downloading and usage of selected high resolution image files. These agencies are in the business of handling—making available for purchase—the preexisting work of photographers. For the most part, photographers provide to these agencies all the work they want them to market. In these relationships, the agencies serve as the agents for the photographers, licensing to others the right to use that work. Most of these agencies develop a reputation for the kind of photographs they have available (celebrities, sports action, travel, etc.), and potential users who need a particular kind of photograph will search their online databases to see what they have. The agencies will send the selected photos to the potential client, and if the client chooses to use one or more, the client and the agency will quickly enter into a contract covering that use or the use will be included in a previously entered into "blanket" agreement.

Such dealings tend to be fairly informal, many based on oral understandings and assumptions. When an agency sends photos to a potential client, it is essentially trusting that client not to use the work until an agreement for that use has been reached and to return or destroy the digital image if no agreement is reached.

Photographers should be careful in selecting the agencies that will handle their work. They should always try to discuss and agree upon the terms governing the relationship, including the scope of the agency's authority to deal with the work (e.g., minimum acceptable fees, unacceptable uses or users, special limits on certain photographs); the agency's compensation for its services (usually at least 50 percent of the generated income); what happens if the work is lost or damaged; credit to be given the photographer when work is used; and the nature and extent of the agency's reporting and payment obligations to the photographer. And whenever possible, the parties should reduce their agreement to a written contract.

What happens when a photographer's work is lost or damaged?

While this used to happen with some regularity, and while many photographers (and agencies) have brought suit in recent years to recover damages for such losses, most professional business transactions involving photos these days are with low or high resolution digital images, thus minimizing the risks of loss or damage. However, where non-digital versions of the work are used, many photographers, encouraged by the American Society of Magazine Photographers, the leading organization representing freelance photographers, attempt to put into their contracts a provision that each photograph lost or damaged is worth at least $1,500 or a similar amount. Most clients, however, will refuse to agree to such provisions, and most courts will not enforce them. Instead, the courts will try to ascertain the true value of the lost or damaged photos, looking to such factors as their uniqueness, their prior income-producing history, and the cost of replacing them.

The photographer or agency will first have to prove which photos were lost or damaged by the client. For this reason, it is crucially important that they keep complete records on all deliveries of their work to others.

What is the role of the photographer's representative?

Many freelance photographers use the services of a photographer's representative ("rep"). In such cases, the terms of the parties' agreement should be discussed and reduced to writing at the beginning of the relationship. Issues such as the rep's responsibilities and authority to speak for and commit the photographer, the compensation to be paid the rep, the reimbursement of the rep's expenses, the rep's reporting and payment obligations, and the circumstances and consequences of a termination of the relationship, should all be clearly spelled out in that contract. If any potential users of the photographer's work are to be excluded from the rep's role (sometimes called "house accounts"), this should also be made clear in the contract.

What happens when the photographer's work is considered fine art?

In addition to the use of photographs in publications and advertising and other commercial vehicles mentioned above, photographs are often sold in galleries and otherwise treated as fine art. For the most part, the applicable contracts are essentially the same as those used in connection with original works of visual art, discussed in the following section.

CONTRACTS INVOLVING VISUAL ARTISTS

Although legally speaking the works of authors and artists have much in common, the differences in work product have led to different legal problems and solutions. Writings of authors are intended to be reproduced and disseminated to as large an audience as possible, and original manuscripts usually have little value. The opposite is true of visual artists: The original often has the most value, and the right to own and control the original may be more important than the right to own and control reproductions. This helps explain the existence of the theories of *droit moral* and *droit de suite* discussed in Chapter 2. This may also explain the differences between the contracts involving visual artists and some of the others we've discussed thus far.

What is the standard contractual relationship between an artist and a gallery?

There are two principal kinds of artist-gallery (or more generally artist-dealer) relationships. In the first the gallery purchases the work of the artist outright and sells it for its own benefit. This happens most often either when the gallery is purchasing on the secondary market or when an artist dies and the estate does not wish to continue to own the artist's works.

In the relationship most common for living artists, the gallery accepts an artist's work on consignment and acts as the artist's agent or representative in seeking to sell it. Laws have been passed in New York and California and many other states governing consignment of artworks to art dealers for exhibition and sale. They provide that unless artwork has been sold outright to a gallery or the artist has received full compensation, the work is deemed on consignment.

How does consignment operate?

Under the New York statute, the dealer is "deemed to be the agent" of such artist, the work of fine art "is trust property in the hands of the consignee [dealer] for the benefit of the consignor [artist]," and "any proceeds from the sale of such work of fine art are trust funds in the hands of the consignee for the benefit of the consignor." The New York statute provides that,

> whenever an artist . . . delivers or causes to be delivered a work of fine art . . . to an art merchant for the purposes of exhibition and/or sale on a commission, fee or other basis of compensation, the delivery to and acceptance thereof by the art merchant establishes a consignor/consignee relationship . . . and such work shall remain trust property notwithstanding its purchase by the consignee for his own account until the price is paid in full to the consignor. If such work is thereafter resold to a bona fide third party before the consignor has been paid in full, the proceeds of the resale are trust funds in the hands of the consignee for the benefit of the consignor to the extent necessary to pay any balance still due to the consignor and such trusteeship shall continue until the fiduciary obligation of the consignee with respect to such transaction is discharged in full.

The statute also provides that a contractual waiver of most of these protections is void.

In states where no statute like New York's has been enacted, the consignment relationship is governed by the law of consigned goods generally. The "fiduciary" and "trust" protections of the New York and California laws are not available, although it is generally believed that the artist-dealer relationship is always one of principal and agent, with the agent assuming fiduciary responsibilities to the artist, especially where there is a significant disparity in business acumen. In those states where no special protection is available, an artist's work in the custody of a gallery can be subject to the claims of the gallery's creditors unless (1) certain notices to the contrary are properly posted, (2) it can be established that the dealer is known by creditors to be engaged in the business of selling the goods of others, and (3) a simple financial statement (known as a "UCC-1 Statement") has been filed (usually electronically) in the appropriate state office. Artists who want the kind of protection afforded by the New York law will have to obtain it in their contracts with their galleries or dealers.

If a gallery is acting as an artist's agent, what should their agreement include?

A gallery will usually insist on the exclusive right to represent the artist's work in a geographic territory. The artist should seek to exclude from exclusive coverage his studio sales, gifts, or barter of his work, although it is not uncommon for the contract to provide for some payment to the gallery even for a private sale by the artist from his studio. The borders of the territory should be carefully spelled out. The agreement should be clear about what works are covered: For example, does it apply only to existing work, or does it include works created after the agreement is entered into? Is the agreement limited to a specific number of works per year, to all of the artist's output in a particular year, or perhaps to the artist's work in one medium? Who chooses from the artist's work, the gallery or the artist? The agreement should always confirm the artist's ownership of the work and that the works are not subject to creditors' claims. It is most important that such questions be fully agreed upon when the contract is made.

The agreement should have a time limit. A short period (e.g., one year) provides the artist with flexibility to upgrade to a more important dealer, but a longer period (e.g., three years) provides the artist with greater security. Many artists seek to impose an annual minimum-sales requirement on the gallery as a condition of keeping the agreement in effect.

If the gallery has branches, the agreement should specify where the work will be displayed. Also, if the artist is relying on a particular person in the gallery to handle the work, the agreement should so specify.

The artist may seek the right to approve, or at least be consulted on, how and where in the gallery her works may be shown and whether some will be on permanent exhibition. The agreement can require a minimum number of exhibitions devoted to the artist during the term of the agreement and can specify the location, opening date, duration, and space for the exhibitions. It can give the artist the right to be present and participate in the hanging, arranging, and lighting of exhibitions. It can specify whether the exhibition will be exclusive or whether other artists' work will also be shown. The artist may desire the right to withdraw from a group show if she does not approve of the other artists.

It is important that the agreement specify who will bear the cost of exhibitions; otherwise, the artist may assume that the gallery will pay while the gallery assumes that the costs will be deducted from the artist's return on sales. The cost and content of promotional and advertising material should also be dealt with in the agreement. Given the increasing importance of art fairs on the market, the agreement should contain similar provisions with respect to art fairs that the gallery or dealer may participate in.

How does the gallery get paid?

Two methods are common. In the "net-price" method the gallery's compensation is the difference between a price agreed between gallery and artist and the price received by the gallery. In the "commission" method, the gallery gets a percentage of the sales price. The problem with the net-price method is that the gallery may profit unconscionably if the artist's work substantially increases in value after the contract price is fixed. Problems with the commission method include the allocation of prices if there are bulk sales and the risk that the gallery may conduct internal sales (i.e., sales to itself). Many artists seek to combine the two methods of payment or seek other remedies to these problems.

How does the gallery price the artist's work?

The agreement should provide for consultation with the artist, if not the artist's prior approval. If prices have been agreed upon, the agreement should also specify under what circumstances and in what percentage the gallery may offer a buyer a discount. Examples include sales to influential collectors or museums, sales of more than one work at a time, or purchases by the dealer on his own account. The prices should be reviewed periodically. The agreement may also deal with rental prices. If the gallery extends credit to purchasers, the agreement should specify whether the payment to the artist is to be based on the amount of the sale or on the money actually received by the gallery, the issue being whether the artist is to participate in the risks and delays inherent in the gallery's decision to grant credit.

CHAPTER 6

BUSINESS AND TAX MATTERS AFFECTING CREATORS

Authors, artists, and other creative people who sell their work or otherwise derive a financial benefit from it are "in business" and must make decisions about the way they conduct their businesses. They are also taxpayers—on the federal, state, and perhaps local level—and should be aware of how tax laws affect them and what steps they can take to minimize their taxes. Also, alas, they will all die and should be concerned about the estates they will leave behind.

A full discussion of these issues is beyond the scope of this chapter. Instead, we will discuss some of the most common business, tax, and estate questions that affect creators.

WAYS OF DOING BUSINESS

An individual creator can conduct business as a sole proprietorship, a corporation, or an LLC. If the creator joins forces with one or more colleagues, an additional method, a partnership, is available.

What is a sole proprietorship, and how is it different from an LLC or a corporation?

A sole proprietorship, the way of doing business used by most creators, simply means that the creator, author, or artist is in business for herself, period. There are no other business entities (except, perhaps, agents or galleries) that stand between such creators and everyone they deal with, including the purchasers of their work.

This is the simplest form of doing business, but it may not be the wisest or the most economical for every creator. A sole proprietor is personally responsible for everything he does, including purchasing supplies, renting a studio, hiring assistants or other staff, and countless other everyday activities. If debts cannot be paid, or if there is an accident in the studio and someone is hurt, or if an assistant defrauds a publisher or a gallery, the sole proprietor may be held personally liable, with creditors or victims collecting what is due from the proprietor's personal income and assets. This unlimited personal liability is a principal reason why many people prefer to do business as an LLC or corporation, where the individual's liability is more limited. If the risks of unlimited liability are not significant or can be insured, an LLC or corporation becomes less attractive.

What about corporations?

Corporations are separate entities for legal and tax purposes, and creators who incorporate must prepare and file official documents with the relevant state agency and must prepare separate tax returns and pay separate taxes for the corporation, apart from their own individual tax returns. But, if they choose to work through a corporation, most individual creators will usually choose to form what is known as an "S" corporation, in which event the corporation's finances are deemed to pass directly to the individual shareholder. S corporations are discussed further below.

What does incorporation entail?

Incorporation involves expenses that a sole proprietorship does not. It is a more cumbersome way of doing business, and many creators will not get significant tax or other benefits from it. Those who are in doubt about whether to incorporate should consult an accountant or lawyer familiar with such matters.

A corporation is in a sense a legal fiction—an entity created by the law that exists only in the eyes of the law. It cannot be seen or touched or talked to. It can conduct business, and hire and fire employees, but only if and when the people who own it tell it to.

Although it is more complicated than a sole proprietorship, a corporation is relatively easy to create. Forming one does not require the services of a lawyer. Essentially, one need only choose a corporate name, make sure the name is available by checking with the appropriate state agency (usually the secretary of state), prepare appropriate documents (the forms for which can usually be obtained from the agency), and deliver them with the necessary fees to the agency.

In most states, it is legal (and common) for a corporation to have only one shareholder, who is also its board of directors and staff. The individual, having formed a corporation, need not involve anyone else in the conduct of its business. To the outside world, she would look no different from the sole proprietorship through which that business was conducted the day before. But to the law and to those with whom the corporation does business, the differences are real and important.

Individual shareholders, directors, and employees of corporations are generally not personally liable for the debts or obligations of the corporation. Creditors, accident victims, or the like can look only to the corporation for satisfaction, and the assets a small corporation has available to provide that satisfaction are usually far more limited than those owned by the individual. In effect, shareholders are insulated from personal liability in many (but not necessarily all) of those situations in which the sole proprietor would be fully liable. There would be no such insulation for accidents actually caused by the individual or where the individual personally guaranteed payment of the corporation's obligations, which is frequently required for small corporations.

The corporate structure works like this: Mary Artist has just formed Mary Artist, Inc. She becomes its only shareholder. As such, she elects the board of directors, which consists solely of herself. As the board of directors, she designates herself as president and secretary (indeed the entire staff) and as the authorized check signer on the corporate bank account. She opens that account in the name of the corporation with a deposit of, say, $250 of her own money, which is treated as payment for the shares of stock issued to her (which is how she became the sole shareholder). A work schedule and salary are agreed upon, with perhaps even a written employment contract, and Mary goes to work. Legally, she now works for the corporation, not herself. The paintings she creates belong to the corporation, which can decide when and for how much to sell them. Proceeds from sales belong to the corporation and are used to pay Mary's salary, the corporate rent, and other bills for her studio and supplies. If any profits remain, they can be applied in a number of ways.

The corporation and Mary must each file a separate income tax return. Mary has to report only the salary she receives from the corporation, and the corporation can deduct that salary from its reported income. It can also deduct many other uses of its income:

for example, employee benefits such as health and life insurance for Mary, placing part of the gross income in profit-sharing or pension plans for Mary's benefit, or mounting an exhibition of Mary's work. In this way, Mary can control her personal reportable income and at the same time enjoy benefits that the corporation can deduct from its taxes, benefits that might not be deductible by Mary if she acquired them as a sole proprietor.

Incorporation can provide meaningful tax benefits in some cases, usually for very successful creators. But such benefits are much less significant, even nonexistent, for the individual creator who has modest income.

What's an LLC?

An LLC—for limited liability company—is a United States–specific form of doing business that combines advantages of a sole proprietorship and of a corporation. Specifically, it provides the "pass-through" financial aspects of a sole proprietorship—i.e., it does not have to prepare its own tax returns or calculate and pay its own separate taxes—with the limited legal liability of a corporation. LLCs do not need to be organized for profit. LLCs are a popular choice of business form for many creative people.

What about partnerships?

Partnerships are essentially sole proprietorships consisting of more than one proprietor. They do not provide the limited liability protection of corporations or LLCs; indeed, each partner can be held liable for obligations incurred by the others in the course of the partnership business. And they do not provide some of the tax advantages available from corporations. But they do enable several persons to pool their resources for their mutual benefit and to share profits and losses in accordance with any formula they choose.

TAX LAWS AND CREATORS

Prior to the Tax Reform Act of 1986, which made significant changes to this country's tax laws, those laws were decidedly unfriendly to creative people. And although that adverse treatment was for a while somewhat alleviated, it has since become clear that that kind of treatment will once again be an unpleasant fact of life for all creators.

Under longstanding provisions of our federal tax law, works created by authors, artists, and other creators are not considered "capital assets" and thus are not entitled to "capital gains" treatment under those laws. More specifically, the law provides that "a copyright, a literary, musical, or artistic composition, a letter or memorandum, or similar property held by . . . a taxpayer whose personal efforts created such property" is ineligible for capital gains treatment. What this means is that when an artist sells a painting or an author grants publishing or movie rights to a book, his income (or "profit," or "gain") from that sale is treated as "ordinary income" for federal tax purposes and not as a "capital gain," which would be the case if the same artist sold a similar work that he purchased from another artist.

Prior to the 1986 changes, the applicable tax rates for ordinary income were substantially higher than for capital gains, and the creator selling her work had to pay taxes on those sales at those much higher rates. The 1986 Act drastically reduced the applicable rates for ordinary income and thus effectively removed the difference between the rates for ordinary income and capital gains. As a result the taxes payable by an artist on the sale of a work would be the same as if the work were considered a capital asset. To that extent, the previous discrepancy in treatment was eliminated.

However, since sales of taxpayer-created works are still denied capital gains treatment, especially to the extent "ordinary income" rates are higher than rates for capital gains, creators who sell or grant rights in their own works will be at a disadvantage, obligated to pay higher taxes (all in the year the income is received) than would be the case if capital gains treatment were available for those sales. In the view of many, the creations of authors, artists, and other creative people, particularly where they have required much time and effort to produce and where their value may appreciate substantially after they are created but before they are sold, should be treated as capital assets.

How are royalties, fees, and other income received by creators treated?

As with the funds received from the sale of a work, funds received by creators as compensation for the grant of rights to a work or for creative services rendered (whether in the form of royalties, fees, salary, profit participation, or otherwise) are also treated as ordinary income in the year such funds are received. This too can create special burdens on creators; for example, an author who puts in ten or even twenty years working on a book, during which she lives on savings or part-time work, and who then enters into a publishing contract with a substantial advance against royalties, has to pay income tax on the full amount of the advance in the year in which it was received, with no ability to "average" that tax over a period of years (as was possible before the Tax Reform Act of 1986).

The "fair market value" of prizes, awards, and the like must be treated as ordinary income. The Tax Reform Act of 1986 significantly restricted the prior rather generous treatment of fellowships and scholarships, under which they were generally excluded from taxes. Now only candidates for degrees can exclude such funds from their reportable income and only to the extent that they are to be used for tuition, fees, books, and supplies required for course work. Any portion of a scholarship or fellowship that represents payment for teaching, research, or other services must be reported as income.

Creators who are self-employed and engaged in a trade or business (discussed further below) are also responsible for the federal self-employment tax that is imposed on all self-employed income, including royalties, for the purposes of old age, survivors, disability, and hospital insurance benefits (Social Security benefits).

What is an S corporation?

Under certain circumstances, a creator can elect to incorporate his business but still be treated for federal tax purposes as an individual and not as a corporation. In this way, he gets the other benefits of incorporation, including limited legal liability, while avoiding the requirements of paying both corporate and individual taxes. There are a number of rules and regulations that must be complied with, but if they can be satisfied choosing S treatment is often a wise course for creators. From a tax perspective, an S corporation will not usually provide tax advantages over a sole proprietorship unless the creator earns income of $500,000 or more.

When are a creator's expenses deductible?

Like all taxpayers, creators (as individuals or corporations) may deduct their "ordinary and necessary expenses incurred during the taxable year in carrying out any trade or business." This presupposes that the creator is engaged in the "trade or business" of creating works. The test is whether the creator's primary purpose and intention in engaging in the activity is to make a profit, and that expectation need not be a reasonable one so long as it is sincere and not a sham. Indeed, one court went out of its way to emphasize that this test would be met even if there was no realistic expectation of profit:

> That the objective, not the expectation, of making a profit is to govern determinations on whether a taxpayer is engaged in a business or a hobby, and the two criteria are not the same. One may embark upon a venture for the sincere purpose of eventually reaping a profit but in the belief that the probability of financial success is small or even remote. He therefore does not really expect a profit, but nonetheless is willing to take the gamble. . . . It cannot be gainsaid that "the activity actually is engaged in for profit"—that it was undertaken "with the objective of making a profit."

Moreover, the absence of income does not prevent an enterprise from being classified as a trade or business. Also, an individual may engage in more than one trade or business. To this extent, the tax laws make it possible for creators to deduct their creative expenses even while they engage in other jobs or professions and even if they don't have income from those creative efforts in the years in which they deduct those expenses.

It is not always easy to know whether a creator will be treated as a trade or business, but the Internal Revenue Code contains a presumption that if gross income exceeded expenses in three of the previous five years, the taxpayer is in business and can deduct expenses.

If the creator qualifies as a trade or business, she can deduct expenses directly from gross income (on Schedule C) without having to itemize them (on Schedule A). This is preferable from a tax point of view to having to treat those expenses as (Schedule A) itemized deductions, which (if the expenses are deductible at all) would be the case if "trade or business" treatment is not available.

What if a creator doesn't qualify as a trade or business?

Even if the creator doesn't qualify as a trade or business, he can deduct expenses incurred in the creation of a work if those expenses are incurred "for the production . . . of income." However, those expenses must be itemized on Schedule A, and creators who do not itemize deductions will not be able to take those deductions. Also, there are specific limits and restrictions on the permissible amounts of such deductions. The Internal Revenue Service has set forth nine factors that are to be considered in determining whether expenses were incurred for the production of income, which factors have been summarized as follows:

> In order for creative activity to qualify as being carried on primarily for the production of income, all the circumstances of the transaction are considered. The taxpayer's intent to produce income from the writing or artistic activity is not by itself sufficient. The relevant factors are the intention of the [creative person], the record of prior gain or loss, the relation between the type of activity and the principal occupation of the individual and the uses to which the writing or artwork is put. Obviously, similarities exist between the criteria for determining if an activity is a trade or business. The difference, however, is in the scope of the activities to be considered.

> The entire enterprise is considered when determining if [a person] is engaged in [a trade or business] . . .

However, a single transaction may be carried on for the production of income. Thus, although qualification under the production of income provision does not have the same tax advantages as qualification under the trade or business provisions, qualification is somewhat easier.

What if a creator's expenses do not qualify for either "trade or business" or "production of income" treatment?

Under such circumstances, the "hobby loss" rules apply. Under those rules, a creator can claim deductions for the expenses incurred while pursuing his or her creative activity, but only to the extent that the gross income derived from that activity during the tax year exceeds the deductions that he or she is otherwise allowed to claim. As with expenses incurred for the production of income, there are limitations and restrictions on the extent to which hobby expenses are deductible. The key factor that indicates that a creator is engaged in a hobby and not a trade or business or working for the production of income is the lack of a bona fide expectation/objective of realizing a profit.

Are there any special requirements for a creator's deductions?

The Tax Reform Act of 1986 attempted to change the way a creator could claim deductions for expenses. Essentially, those changes required creators to keep elaborate records of their expenses and to allocate those expenses to the various works on which they were incurred. Thus, somehow an author had to allocate among her works her expenses for typing paper or computer disks, and an artist had to allocate her expenses for paints, brushes, and easels. These changes were strongly protested by creators and their organizations, and by 1988 they were substantially alleviated.

Under legislation enacted that year, those allocation requirements do not apply to "qualified creative expenses" incurred by "freelance authors, photographers, and artists." Those expenses are defined as any expense "which is paid or incurred by an individual in the trade or business of such individual (other than as an employee) of being a writer, photographer, or artist, and . . . which, without regard to this section, would be allowable as a deduction for the taxable year." That section contains definitions of the terms "writer," "photographer," and artist": "any individual if the personal efforts of such individual create (or may reasonably be expected to create)" a "literary manuscript . . . a photograph or photographic negative or transparency . . . [or] a picture, painting, sculpture, statue, etching, drawing, cartoon, graphic design, or original print edition."

What kinds of expenses are deductible?

To be deductible, expenses must be "ordinary and necessary." This requirement has been described as follows:

> That is, in general, they must be normal, usual, and customary in the business in which the individual is involved, whether one is an author or in any other business. Ordinary might be defined as an expense that arises with some degree of consistency in the business of the individual involved, and necessary means that it is appropriate or helpful to the development or conduct of the trade or business. I think there is one other criterion that the expense would probably have to satisfy—it must be reasonable. Assuming that all of these three criteria were established, the expense would be deductible against the current income of the individual involved.

Many expenses incurred by creators are clearly deductible. These would include expenses for supplies and equipment; travel and lodging expenses while on business; rent, utilities, and other office- or studio-related expenses; and salaries, fees, and other payments made to assistants, models, and others. Similarly, fees paid to agents, representatives, galleries, and the like would be deductible. But other expenses may be more questionable, including especially those for a home office and for entertainment. Now, only 80 percent of expenses incurred for meals and entertainment expenses are deductible, and only if the expense was "directly related" to "the active conduct of the taxpayer's trade or business."

To be able to deduct expenses for a home office, the Code requires that (1) the space be used exclusively for business; (2) it be used for business purposes on a regular basis; (3) it must be the principal place of the business being conducted there; and (4) the taxpayer cannot deduct expenses that exceed the gross income from the business use, so that if there is no income, there can be no such deductions.

Expenses incurred for taking courses and attending conferences will be deductible if they are intended to maintain or improve the creator's work, but not if their only purpose is to enable the individual to become a creator.

What if a creator wants to donate a work to charity?

A creator is free to donate works to charitable organizations. However, because the works of a creator are not considered capital assets, tax laws impose severe restrictions on the amount the creator can claim as the value of the work contributed. Essentially, the value will be limited to the amounts actually expended by the artist in the creation of the work (i.e., his "cost basis" in the work). Thus, even if the work is worth thousands or perhaps millions of dollars in the marketplace, the creator may claim only his actual costs for the work. As a result, there is a real and unfortunate disincentive to creators to donate works to charitable organizations.

What can creators do to minimize tax burdens?
First, they should keep detailed records of their deductible expenses, including reference to the business purpose of the expense if it is not self-evident. If they don't and there is an audit, the claimed deductions may be disallowed.

Second, they can take advantage of tax-saving programs that are available to all. For example, sums placed in SEP (for Simplified Employee Pension) retirement plans or IRA (Individual Retirement Accounts) plans are deductible from current income and are not taxable until the individual takes them out, usually at retirement when income and tax rates are presumably lower. The appreciation of and income earned on the funds are not taxable until the money is taken out. There are maximum limits for annual contributions—much higher for SEPs than for IRAs—and beginning at age seventy and one-half the creator must withdraw a specified amount (Required Minimum Distribution) that will be treated as taxable ordinary income, whatever the creator's actual financial circumstances.

Third, they can take steps to control the income they receive in a given year. An author can arrange with a publisher, or an artist with a gallery, not to be paid more than a fixed amount in a given year. If tax is paid on the "cash basis" (income as received, which is what most taxpayers do), there will be no tax on income not yet paid by the publisher or gallery. Such arrangements may minimize tax exposure, but they have drawbacks: It is unlikely that the publisher or gallery will agree to pay interest, or enough interest, on sums held, and the creator will lose money because of this; also, the publisher or gallery may go out of business or otherwise become insolvent and be unable to pay.

Finally, creators can transfer works and/or some or all of their copyright interests in works to other people by what the law calls *inter vivos* (between living people) transfers. Under current law, gifts of up to $14,000 (in cash or other assets) to any recipient in any year can be made without any gift tax liability. If correctly done, such transfers can not only shift the tax liability for the income or gains subsequently realized from those works from the donor (giver) to the donee (receiver) but also reduce the value (and tax liability) of the creator's estate at the time of her death (discussed further below). However, it should be noted that as a result of the Tax Reform Act of 1986, it is no longer possible to obtain income tax advantages by transferring works or rights to minor children since that law provided that the net unearned income of a child under the age of fourteen in excess of a relatively nominal amount is subject to tax at the top marginal rate of the child's parents.

What can a corporation do to minimize taxes?

Corporations, at least those with limited income, generally pay lower tax rates than individuals. Moreover, corporations pay taxes only on profits (i.e., the amount that remains after payments for salaries, other expenses, and retirement investments, etc.). With proper planning, it is possible that the corporation will pay little or no tax and that the creator will pay significantly less tax than he would have paid as a sole proprietor. However, as the taxable income of the corporation increases, which means that the applicable tax rate also increases, the amount of total tax savings will decrease, and the tax benefits of incorporation become less significant.

The corporation can control the amount it pays the individual each year, thus providing better foreknowledge and control of the individual's taxable income. The corporation can also control when sums are paid (e.g., as salary or dividends) so that they are received at a time most advantageous to the creator. (There are also tax advantages on "fringe" benefits, as discussed earlier in the chapter.)

Finally, corporations can create pension and profit-sharing plans to defer and minimize taxes. Like individuals' SEP and IRA plans, these plans segregate and invest moneys on which the employee does not have to pay taxes until later. Since 1982, the amount of money that may be placed in tax-deferred pension plans is the same for individuals and corporations.

These proposals are fraught with technical requirements that must be complied with. The services of an accountant or lawyer will probably be necessary. If done properly, they can bring significant savings to the creative person.

What about foreign income?

Creators will sometimes earn income outside the United States—for example, an author whose book is published in other countries will earn royalties from those sales. Usually, the foreign publisher will deduct from the sums otherwise payable to the author the amount needed to satisfy the author's tax obligation to the country where the sums are earned, and then send a statement showing the deduction along with the remaining payment due. In preparing the author's U.S. tax returns, some authors only declare the net amount actually received, while others report the "gross"—pre-deduction—amount earned, and then claim as an allowed deduction the foreign taxes that were deducted from that gross. Tax experts advise that the latter option tends to be in the author's best tax interests.

THE CREATOR'S ESTATE

Estate problems, particularly those of artists, are significant. As one commentator has noted:

> The accumulated life's work of the working artist is [most] troubling. Most working artists do not focus on the problems that will be presented to their estate in disposing of their work in an effective way. If the artist has achieved limited public acceptance prior to death, the issue is not a major one. The Internal Revenue Service may ignore concern as to the value of the work for estate tax purposes and may permit a modest estate the value claimed without any dispute. If, however, the artist had publicly reported sales in any significant numbers, the problem can be acute, and if the family of the artist has any concern in perpetuating the name of the artist—and generating any significant proceeds by the sale of his work—the problem can be severe and the methods of solving the problem can have substantial disparate results.

The problem is that for federal estate tax purposes, the assets of the decedent must be valued as of the date of death (or six months thereafter). If an artist leaves a significant number of works, including many that may have been created years earlier, difficult and crucial issues of valuation are presented. How is the "fair market value" of those works to be determined? The answer to that question can often spell the difference between a devastating estate-tax exposure and one that can be managed.

A high estate tax will create severe burdens and pressures on the estate, which may be forced to sell works immediately to pay the tax. Naturally, a forced sale does not maximize the income of the estate, nor does it otherwise positively serve the reputation and future value of the work. The Internal Revenue Code has provisions that would enable an estate to defer the payment of estate taxes under certain circumstances, particularly if specified percentages of the estate are attributable to a "closely held business."

The applicable estate-tax rates—indeed whether there should be any estate tax at all (opponents of the tax call it the "death tax")—are the subject of intense political debate, and those interested in the current rate—and the applicable exemptions, etc.—should consult their lawyer or accountant for that information. As this is written, under the "marital exemption"— the inheritance of a surviving spouse that will be exempt from estate tax—now provides that the entire inheritance is exempt. This means that there will be no estate tax payable when the first spouse dies, with the full estate tax payable on the survivor's estate at the time of that spouse's death.

When created works are inherited, the tax "basis" for those works is their value at the time of inheritance. This means that any appreciation in the value of those works prior to the creator's death will not be the tax responsibility of the person inheriting the work; that person will have to pay tax only on the amount of the increase in the value of the work after the creator's death when that work is sold by the person inheriting the work.

What about copyrights in a creator's estate?

As was discussed in Chapter 2, ownership of a work does not automatically include ownership in the copyright in that work, and vice versa. As a result, creators and their estate planners should take special care in disposing of the copyrights in works as well as the works themselves, and it should be remembered that the work can go to one recipient (perhaps a museum) and the copyright in the work to another heir entirely.

As also discussed in Chapter 2, under some circumstances the U.S. Copyright Act may override provisions in a creator's will. In such cases, the Copyright Act spells out who will be entitled to the copyright—and to the right to terminate certain grants— regardless of the provisions of the creator's will.

What should creators do to plan their estates?

All creative people, but especially those who may leave sizable estates on their death, should plan ahead for the disposition of their work and the payment of estate taxes when they die. They should have wills that dispose of their estates in an orderly way consistent with their desires, and they should have those wills planned and drafted by professionals who are knowledgeable and experienced in the special problems presented by the estates of creators. They should also consider transfers or gifts during their lifetime that may serve the best interests of their families and their work, including to trusts. But special care should be taken not to appoint persons with authority over the works who may have a conflict of interest with respect to the work, such as the creator's publisher or gallery owner.

ACKNOWLEDGMENTS

Several colleagues graciously reviewed portions of this book and provided invaluable suggestions; the book has been significantly enhanced by their contributions. My sincere thanks to Elliott Brown, Robert Pesce, Chris Robinson, Steve Sheppard, and Jeffrey Smith. I also want to thank the friends, clients, and colleagues who (more or less) cheerfully allowed themselves to be induced to provide their far too generous endorsements for the book.

Both the American Civil Liberties Union, the publisher of the predecessor editions of this book, and Jerry Simon Chasen, my co-author of those editions, facilitated this expanded and updated edition, and I am pleased to acknowledge their cooperation.

It has been a pleasure to work with the folks at Page Street Publishing, whose patience, tact, enthusiasm, and expertise never flagged and who made it possible to transform this book from an idea into an actual physical (and digital) reality. Most conspicuously, those folks include Will Kiester, Meg Palmer, Marissa Giambelluca, Karen Levy, Patricia Kot, and Jill Browning. Many thanks to you all!

Cooper Knowlton, who maintains his own law practice and is "Of Counsel" to my firm, gave me the support to undertake this edition. It would not have happened without him. I am delighted to acknowledge his contribution in the byline of the book.

Finally, my heartfelt and perpetual thanks and awe to my wife, Helen Baldassare, who both indulged my absorption in the project ("I'm writing a book!") and provided support and input.

Ken Norwick, 2017

ABOUT THE AUTHOR

Ken Norwick is a nationally recognized lawyer and authority on intellectual property, communications, publishing, and media law. His clients have included His Holiness the Dalai Lama, Garrison Keillor, Terry Southern, Mitch Albom, Kimberla Lawson Roby, Robert Pirsig, Annie Leibovitz, Veterans of Foreign Wars of the United States, and the Humane Society of the United States, as well as *Playboy, Working Woman, The Comics Journal*, and *Men's Fitness* magazines. He is general counsel to the Association of Authors' Representatives, the national organization of literary agents. He is the author of numerous books and articles on legal and political subjects, including *The Rights of Authors, Artists and Other Creative People*, on which this book is based. He has taught publishing and constitutional law and has served as legislative director of the New York Civil Liberties Union and as a consultant to the American Civil Liberties Union. He is a member of the Authors Guild and the Media Law Resource Center and has been named a New York "Super Lawyer."

INDEX